COMMITTEE FOR ECONOMIC DEVELOPMENT
RESEARCH STUDY

PRODUCTION, JOBS AND TAXES

THE BOARD OF TRUSTEES

RESEARCH COMMITTEE

COMMITTEE FOR ECONOMIC DEVELOPMENT
RESEARCH STUDY

PRODUCTION, JOBS AND TAXES

Postwar Revision of the Federal Tax System to Help Achieve Higher Production and More Jobs

BY

HAROLD M. GROVES

Professor of Economics, University of Wisconsin

FIRST EDITION

McGRAW-HILL BOOK COMPANY, INC.

NEW YORK AND LONDON

1944

THE MAPLE PRESS COMPANY, YORK, PA.

FOREWORD

THIS study of postwar federal tax policy is the first of a
series of research reports to be published under the auspices
of the Research Committee of the Committee for Economic
Development. The C.E.D. hopes that these studies when
completed will provide a well-rounded analysis of the economic problems involved in attaining and maintaining new
high levels of employment through expanded production after
the war.

The research program of the C.E.D. is unique in this country. It is based on a cooperative undertaking between
businessmen and scholars. Responsibility for the development and supervision of the program is vested in a *Research
Committee,* composed entirely of businessmen. A *Research
Advisory Board,* composed of distinguished social scientists,
assists the Research Committee in planning and supervising
the research program, and is given final authority to approve
for publication all of the research studies. A full-time
Research Director, Theodore O. Yntema, is in charge of the
research staff and is responsible for the selection of the
specialists in each particular field of investigation and for
supervising the preparation of research studies.

In accordance with these procedures, the Research Committee early in 1943 authorized a group of research studies
under the general heading of "*Taxation and Business:* Studies of
Incentives for Business Enterprise and the Impact of Taxation
on These Incentives." This group of studies was placed under
the direction of C. E. Griffin, Dean of the School of Business
Administration, University of Michigan. At the suggestion
of Dean Griffin, Harold M. Groves, Professor of Economics,
University of Wisconsin, was engaged to head the study of
postwar federal tax revision, and Henry C. Simons, Associate
Professor of Economics, University of Chicago, and William
A. Paton, Professor of Economics and Accounting, University
of Michigan, were employed as consultants.

Foreword

The following report by Professor Groves has been prepared under the supervision of Research Director Yntema and has been approved by a reading committee of the Research Advisory Board. Professor Groves, however, is solely responsible for the opinions and conclusions presented in his study. He has had the benefit of numerous criticisms and suggestions by members of the Research Committee and by other members of the research staff. He has been entirely free, however, to accept or reject any or all suggestions by others in accordance with his own judgment. Similarly, the members of the Research Committee and the members of the Board of Trustees of C.E.D. in sponsoring the publication of this study do not thereby accept responsibility for the views expressed therein or by implication endorse its conclusions.

Soon after the publication of this study, the Research Committee will publish a policy statement on postwar federal taxation in a pamphlet entitled "Postwar Employment and Federal Taxation." This pamphlet represents the views of the members of the Research Committee of businessmen; for which they are solely responsible. The Committee in the development of this statement has benefited greatly from the work of Professor Groves and other members of the research staff, but none of the latter will have any responsibility for the views expressed therein.

The philosophy underlying the policy statement by the Research Committee will be basically the same as that expressed by Professor Groves. The policy statement will contain some specific recommendations which differ in minor respects from those proposed by Professor Groves. The differences will be explained in footnotes in the policy statement. The Committee believes that Professor Groves's study represents an outstanding contribution to the subject of taxation, and with certain minor exceptions, it approves its conclusions and recommendations.

RALPH E. FLANDERS, Chairman
Research Committee

CONTENTS

Contents

Contents

INTRODUCTION

THE founders of the Committee for Economic Development had the vision to provide for unbiased study of the economic problems involved in the attainment of high levels of employment and production. They specified that all research should be thoroughly objective in character and that the approach in each instance should be from the standpoint of the general welfare and not from that of any special political or economic group. To implement this policy, they also stipulated in the by-laws that the Research Director should have control of the selection of research personnel and that the approval or disapproval of a report for publication should rest solely with a committee chosen from the social scientists composing the Research Advisory Board. In practice, the members of this committee base their votes entirely on the general technical competence of the study; their approval for publication does not imply endorsement of all the author's conclusions and recommendations.

This is the first of the reports produced under these conditions. As the author has indicated, we are indebted to many persons for assistance and advice. In particular, the joint discussions by the Research Committee of businessmen and the Research Advisory Board of economists have been most stimulating and helpful.

The research program of the Committee for Economic Development includes several studies of postwar transition problems and several studies of long-run, fundamental problems in achieving a high level of employment and production. A list of these will be found on page 110. It is the hope and endeavor of the Research Staff to contribute to straight thinking on these crucial issues of economic policy.

THEODORE O. YNTEMA
Research Director

PREFACE

THIS report summarizes the major findings of part of a larger study of taxation and incentives now in progress. It deals only with certain aspects of federal postwar tax problems. The final report will cover other aspects of the subject, including estimates of specific postwar financial requirements, recommended rates and exemptions, the incidence of the proposed tax system, quantitative characteristics of the income-tax base in relation to the national income, incentive tax proposals, and state and local taxation. The general outline of the recommendations here presented may be considered conclusive, but the details are tentative and subject to revision in the final report.

This project has been almost a collective undertaking, and full acknowledgment of contributions is impossible. Theodore O. Yntema, Research Director of the Committee for Economic Development, rendered invaluable assistance both in an advisory and an editorial capacity. Professors Henry C. Simons and William A. Paton as consultants and Dean Clare Griffin as business administrator and consultant supplied many excellent suggestions. The Research Committee, the Research Advisory Board, and the staff of the Committee for Economic Development discussed the report in its various stages of preparation, and this constant interchange of ideas proved most helpful. Many persons, including several members of these groups, read the manuscript to its great improvement. Acknowledgment of further assistance is due Sylvia Stone and Marion Goetz for editorial revision and Oscar Litterer and Edith Green for research assistance.

While acknowledging these many contributions, the author assumes responsibility for the ideas here expressed.

HAROLD M. GROVES

MADISON, WIS.,
April, 1944.

I. SUMMARY OF MAJOR RECOMMENDATIONS AND CONCLUSIONS

1. In recasting the federal tax system after the war, particular attention should be given to the development and preservation of adequate business incentives. This is essential because of the paramount interest in developing high levels of production and employment opportunity. These high levels will require, too, the maintenance of an adequate market. Attention to other fundamental interests, such as fairness and adequacy of revenue, is also necessary. A sound and sensible tax program must be based on a proper balance of all these interests.

2. The duplication in corporate and personal income taxes should be eliminated by integrating the two levies. This can be done by confining the corporation tax to a withholding levy on dividends and an advance payment on income retained by the corporation for reinvestment. (The advance payment would be credited to the stockholder to apply on his personal tax liability if and when dividends were distributed or a capital gain were to occur through realization on the reinvestment when stock is transferred.) To avoid precipitous adjustments, the change could be made in several steps over a period of years.

The elimination of this duplication in corporate and personal taxes would result in a reduction of prices, or an increase in wages, or an increase in the peacetime rate of corporate profits, or some combination of these effects. Any or all of these results would encourage expansion of investment, output, and employment. Business incentives are impeded more by taxes imposed on business as such than by personal taxes levied on the investor.

· 1 ·

The advance payment on retained income at the withholding rate would constitute current payment, in part, of personal taxes on such income. It would exert no pressure against the reinvestment of corporate earnings.

While this proposal may be regarded as calling for the elimination of the corporate tax, it may also be viewed as a reduction in personal taxes to the extent that they overlap corporation taxes.

The change here recommended is supported by considerations of equity as well as by those of output. The argument to the contrary is based mainly on the untenable notion that inanimate objects can bear taxes.

3. An exemption from the advance payment on retained income, in the case of new independent manufacturing enterprises of small size, should be provided (see page 44). This would help foster new investment and new competition. It would aid small business in raising equity capital, a process in which it is now handicapped by a serious competitive disadvantage. This exemption could not be called a subsidy since, in the first place, it would involve only a postponement of taxes and, in the second place, it would correct an unfair competitive disadvantage rather than create an unfair competitive advantage. Many of the other changes here recommended would also be especially helpful to small and new enterprises. Provided that it does not subsidize smallness or penalize size as such, the tax system should be used insofar as feasible to ease the special difficulties of small business.

4. The excess-profits tax should be repealed soon after the end of the war, the repeal to take effect a year later. A peacetime excess-profits tax would penalize risk taking, managerial efficiency, and irregularity of income. As a means of recapturing monopoly profits, it would be too crude an instrument to be recommended, and it might actually encourage monopoly. Profits taxes become incredibly complex and involve heavy compliance costs. Postponement of the effec-

tive date of repeal would afford opportunity to continue inflation-control measures while they are necessary.

5. The declared-value capital-stock excess-profits tax combination should be repealed now. It adds nothing of positive value to the tax system, is inimical to small companies, and represents the kind of complication that might well be avoided in the future.

6. A carry-over of at least six years for net business losses should be allowed. Without such allowance, many income taxes are paid out of capital rather than income, as they often were during most of the depression years of the thirties when no carry-over at all was permitted. Fear of losses is often more of an impediment to business expansion than doubt concerning adequate positive profits. Allowance for losses should apply to unincorporated as well as incorporated business.

7. More latitude in the timing of deductions for depreciation and obsolescence of plant and equipment should be allowed. The calculation of these expenses involves so many variables and unknowns that no precise determination is possible. Less attention should be paid to the calendar year in accounting for income-tax purposes. This in itself would reduce the argument and litigation over the proper amounts of depreciation and obsolescence to be charged against the operations of any one period. Shortening the write-off period for these impairments of capital promotes economic progress by reducing resistance to the installation of improved equipment. Accelerated depreciation (as in the present 5-year amortization provision for certain war capital) could be used to promote investment during a depression, and, in extreme cases, its use for such purposes is recommended.

8. The personal income tax should be the mainstay of the postwar federal revenue system. A broad base and a high standard rate should be maintained after the war, and these features should be supported by withholding and by much stronger administration. Present rates and exemptions are

TxU

· 3 ·

little if any above the levels that should have been applied before the war. The tax load for families in the lower income groups should be lightened by eliminating or reducing federal sales taxes. At present levels of federal excises, this relief can be substantial. A shift from business to personal taxes, by bringing tax burdens into the open and by extending the scope of the personal tax with its exemptions and progressive rates, will also benefit the recipients of lower incomes. Under the modifications here proposed, the tax system would be more widely and more positively progressive than it was before the war.

9. Some moderation is warranted in the personal tax schedule as it applies to the upper and middle levels of income, where top rates are now as high as 90 per cent. To be consistent with the social interest in the investment of high incomes in risk-bearing securities, these rates should be reduced by a quarter or a third, or the higher rates should be confined to levels of income at which relatively small amounts of potential capital exist. More would be accomplished by plugging known loopholes in income taxation than by setting surtax rates so high that they defeat themselves. Some restraint in reducing surtaxes is required, however, if maintenance of an adequate standard rate is to win support. Substantial progression in surtaxes is needed to give due weight to the valid interest in less inequality of income. It may seem unfair to call for the maintenance of standard rates at wartime levels and, at the same time, a reduction in surtax rates, but this recasting of relative rates is needed to correct a lopsided scale that prevailed before the war. Some compensation for the unbalanced revision can be made by strengthening death taxes and by eliminating income-tax loopholes.

10. Tax exemption for income from government securities should be eliminated. The tax-exemption feature favors the most riskless investment. The principle of universality in the personal income tax, calling for the inclusion of all types of

income in the base and measure of the tax, should be respected with as few exceptions as possible. The interests of two groups—state and local governments and present security holders—prevent plugging this loophole. Because of the artificial demand created for their securities by tax exemption, state and local governments are able to obtain their loan funds at very low rates of interest. Consequently, they oppose any change. Security holders who have purchased low-yielding state and local bonds on the assumption that the privileged status of these securities would continue also defend existing immunities. Interest on federal bonds (except on those issued before 1941, on which the federal government is bound by contract until a refunding occurs) is now taxable under the federal law. Compensation for these vested interests might take the form of an allowance to state and local governments for increased interest required on new issues or an allowance to security holders to supplement interest payments, making up for the reduced interest attributable to the tax exemption now canceled. If such compensation should be necessary to rid us of tax-exempt bonds, the outlay would be well warranted. Ending tax exemption on new issues would be a step forward, but complete elimination of the exemption privilege is highly desirable.

11. There should be no segregation or other limitation on the deductibility of capital losses, and net losses occasioned by such deductibility should be subject to carry-over privileges. Either by averaging income over a period of years or by other feasible provisions (see pages 80, 85, 86), due allowance should be made for the fact that capital gains and losses often accrue over long periods; they should not be treated as though they rose from a single year's operations. (A longer span for reckoning income-tax liability would also reduce tax avoidance by manipulation of capital losses.) A capital gain attributable to the reinvestment of corporate income is the equivalent of a delayed or liquidating dividend. Due credit should therefore be allowed for taxes already paid by the

corporation on such income. If adequate provisions are enacted for the averaging of personal income over a period of years, if full credit is allowed for corporate taxes on undistributed profits, and if personal surtax rates are reduced to reasonable levels, then capital gains *and losses* can, and should, be treated for tax purposes like other income. Until these basic modifications, here recommended, are made in the tax laws, some form of segregation and special treatment of capital gains and losses will be desirable.

Transfers at death or by gift should be considered as a realization of a gain or loss. Windfalls that might result from the sale of stocks at prices increased as a result of the integration of the corporate and personal income taxes would be fully subject to the income tax as capital gains.

12. The personal income tax should provide some periodic adjustments to eliminate or at least mitigate the discrimination against the recipient of fluctuating as compared with stable income. The present system with its progressive rates greatly overtaxes the incomes of individuals whose earnings may be very high in one year and moderate or very low in another year. A system for mitigating this evil is here outlined (see pages 85 to 86). That it adds a complication to the income tax cannot be denied. But the complication is well worth its cost and could be offset by many simplifications that would involve little or no sacrifice of important interests.

13. For death-tax purposes, estates should be appraised at their value at death or the amount realized in liquidation, whichever is lower. There would then be less reason for shifting investments to liquid assets in anticipation of the estates tax.

14. Death taxes can and should be strengthened by plugging loopholes and by broadening the base of these levies. Estate and gift taxes should be integrated. Death taxes probably affect business incentives less than do immediate personal income taxes. Some strengthening of the estates tax

can be regarded as a desirable offset for a reduction in income surtaxes.

15. Postwar federal sales taxes, especially those on the necessities of life, are to be discouraged. They are objectionable from the standpoint of equity and threaten the enlarged market essential for the maintenance of high-level postwar employment. By avoiding the personal discipline required in direct taxes, they are conducive to governmental extravagance.

16. The experience-rating feature of pay roll taxes (see pages 95–96) levied for unemployment compensation provides a desirable incentive for stabilization of employment. This should not be eliminated by either state or federal action.

17. The 2-year carry-back of losses and the excess-profits-tax credit provided by the Revenue Act of 1942 should be retained in effect even though the excess-profits tax is repealed. This is mainly in accord with the view that the measure of war profits should include war-caused postwar expenditures. Allowance of refunds before the end of the war, in cases where need and validity of present or future claim are established, would facilitate reconversion. A modification of the carry-back system, permitting war-caused postwar expenses to be carried back directly (rather than as losses and profits-tax credits), should be given consideration. These changes would not preclude any sound development of allowances for specific reserves, such as for the fluctuation in the value of inventories. Allowance of these reserves and carry-backs is not a matter of avoiding taxes on war-caused or wartime profits but an attempt to appraise such earnings correctly.

18. An adequate fiscal program to avoid inflation both during and after the war is of paramount importance to business stability. To conserve the deferred purchasing power essential to postwar prosperity, prices must be kept under control. While no analysis of this problem in detail is presented here, it is apparent that a pay-as-you-go federal budget program now would facilitate reconversion and the mainte-

nance of high levels of employment and production after the war.

19. During the first few months after the close of the war, tax reductions, if any, should be conservative. This would ensure that tax changes would not aggravate an inflation problem. In the period following, during which the economy will probably be subjected to its greatest strain of reorganization, the major modifications in the postwar tax system should be made. These modifications should counteract any tendencies toward diffidence. The peacetime budget should be balanced at reasonably high levels of income and employment, and it should at times produce a surplus.

20. The modifications here recommended would work toward a tax system without duplication of taxes, moderate as to degree, universal in application, and free from special privileges. It is believed that a sensible and well-balanced tax system is the best "incentive taxation."

II. INTRODUCTION

1. TAXES AND INCENTIVES

ALMOST all economic thinking about the future starts with the vital need for high postwar levels of production and employment. As to this point, the Keynesians and the orthodox economists, the Beveridge Report and the National Association of Manufacturers—all are agreed. Our common objective is high, and progressively higher, standards of living and, as a means to this end, maximum opportunity to work and to engage in productive enterprise.

The need for a high national income is apparent also in our public finances. Without stopping to itemize the account, we can accept as reasonable the estimates that our postwar federal expenditures will amount to some 20 billion dollars annually. This is huge in comparison with an outlay of 9 billion dollars in 1939 and the maximum tax-raising achievement in any peacetime year (barring 1941) of 6 billion dollars in 1938.

On the other hand, we now have a federal tax system capable of producing currently some 42 billion dollars of revenue. Moreover, part of the wartime tax structure is definitely of an emergency character. This means that a postwar overhauling of the tax system is both feasible and inevitable.

In postwar tax reform it would be unwise to try to concoct a panacea for our economic ills. Such an attempt would do little to correct, and in fact would help to perpetuate, other fundamental maladjustments. Plans involving discriminatory rates of taxation or special concessions to special classes of income would lead us where all efforts at special dispensations lead—to administrative complexities and political log-rolling.

Taxation does influence production. By its effects on the motives that lead individuals or groups into production, it may become a rein or a spur. The effects may be positive if—in the face of new taxation—taxpayers exert more initiative, energy, and inventiveness in order to maintain standards. Taxation may, however, by design or ineptitude, discourage initiative. Few propositions in public finance have more often been cited than the one which tells us that "the power to tax is the power to destroy." By its relative weight on one form of economic activity as compared with another, taxation may influence the choice of alternatives. If our objective is a dynamic and an expanding economy, our tax system should not discourage new ventures and the taking of risks.[1]

Giving particular attention to the impact of taxation upon production and employment does not mean neglecting other objectives of taxation, such as fairness or equity, or the adequacy of revenue yield. A sensible tax program must be based on a balance of all these considerations. Fairness, or equity, in taxation calls for reasonable classification and like treatment of those in like circumstances. Beyond this, the term is associated with the concept of ability to pay or with a frank interest in reducing inequalities in the distribution of income or wealth. It cannot be denied that the desire for "equity" will at times conflict with concern for incentives. High surtaxes on personal income are a clear case of this conflict. Where opposing interests clash, compromise becomes necessary. But there are a surprising number of important tax reforms that involve no clash of interests at all and that can be recommended in the name of both equity and incentives. Usually there is no conflict between a tax program that nurtures production and one that seeks adequate revenues.

---

[1] Of course, there is a distinction between gains that constitute a reward for wealth-creating activities and acquisition that occurs without the performance of any socially useful function. A sound tax system need have solicitude only for the former.

2. HYPOTHESES CONCERNING TAXATION
AND INCENTIVES

The motives that lead men to venture their earnings and their abilities in new undertakings are not easily catalogued. They are a blend of psychological and social, as well as economic, interests. Not all profit is monetary. Here we are mainly concerned with economic motivation. Much of what we know about this necessarily comes from observation and opinion which is not rigorously scientific. On the basis of such evidence, the following hypotheses are offered:

1. Other things being equal, the higher the degree of taxation the more likely it is to affect economic motivation adversely. Certainly far less concern for incentives is required when taxation amounts to one-eighth the national income than when it amounts to one-fourth.

2. The *form* as well as the *degree* of taxation is important. Everyone knows that by skillful adjustment of a pack to the right location upon his back a hiker can carry a load that would otherwise be unbearable. Proper techniques of taxation can likewise reduce its burden and its harmful effects upon the economy.

3. Taxes levied directly upon business concerns as such are likely to restrain business activity more than taxes upon individuals. The significance of corporate production and of management divorced from ownership must here be given due consideration. The interest of management in building a successful business may serve effectively as motivation even though the possibility of high net personal rewards to the stockholder is considerably limited. The effect of taxes on managerial decisions will be certainly less direct and probably less substantial if levies are imposed on shareholders rather than on their companies. Managements will be rated and rewarded by what they deliver in terms of company earnings and not by what these gains mean net of tax to stockholders.

4. Fear of losses is often of more concern to the businessman than the hope of a very high positive profit.

5. The rate of tax on the marginal portion of profits or other income—the top bracket—may be of greater importance than the average effective rate of taxation. The application of the excess-profits tax at the margin is a case in point. This tax may not represent a high proportion of net income because of the credits allowed and because of the bracket system of graduation; but on any additional increment to income the tax may bear with great severity. It is the net increment of income after tax which is of vital importance in motivation, and it is the decision to seek or not to seek that increment which affects the volume of employment and production. (Thus a 90 per cent profits tax on the income in excess of a 10 per cent return on capital may amount to very little in the aggregate for a concern that has an 11 per cent return, but it may discourage that company conclusively from seeking a return of 12 per cent.)

6. The motivation to risk and initiate is probably more sensitive to attack than the motivation to work and manage. Leisure competes with work, to be sure, but liquid and relatively secure investments compete with more venturesome undertakings more effectively. Of course, the element of gambling is often attractive and the available supply of venturers is usually amazingly large even though the chance for success in a given line of enterprise is slight and the mortality rate high. Probably the average rate of profit in venturesome undertakings need not be high. But there must be some substantial prizes to be won.

7. Other things being equal, uncertainty and the frequent change of the tax laws are inimical to business activity. In this connection it may be observed that the federal tax laws have been overhauled some eighteen times in the last thirty years. Some of this is the price we pay for democracy. And while one is suggesting further modifications, one cannot stand too staunchly for a program of leaving tax laws undisturbed!

Nevertheless, a presumption favoring stability in taxation may be recognized. Retroactive changes, precluding the possibility of corresponding business adjustments, are particularly bad.

8. Commitments for business expansion depend on anticipation of the future. Present experience is important mainly as an indication of future prospects. Tax reductions which are definitely expected may be as stimulating as those which are already realized.

9. Ordinarily, a tax program will facilitate production if it leaves business decisions as much as possible to business discretion. Tax consequences enter very heavily into many business decisions at the present time. The decisions to operate as a corporation or a partnership, to distribute dividends or reinvest earnings, to finance with stocks or bonds, and so on, are all likely to be greatly influenced by "advice of counsel" as to the tax consequences. Much of this influence is without any claim to a desirable social objective, although there are, no doubt, cases where the modification of business behavior at the behest of the tax system is in the social interest. The tax system cannot be entirely neutral in its effects on business decisions, but a strong presumption in favor of as little interference as necessary may be recognized. Tax preferments as well as penalties are suspect. In any case, this is not the time to plant a new crop of tax subsidies when the principal task is to weed out the discriminations (largely unintended) in the tax system as it stands.

During recent years considerable support for "incentive taxation" has developed. This term is used to cover a variety of proposals providing preferred treatment for income from business enterprise and establishing rewards and penalties considered appropriate to stimulate output. Some of these proposals might accomplish their objectives, but in general they do not seem promising for the following reasons:

1. The economic system in its normal operation should generate opportunities and incentives for enterprise. If,

under a fair and sensible tax system, it fails to do so, the real causes of difficulty should be sought out and the appropriate remedies applied.[1]

2. A system of bounties and penalties, politically chosen and imposed, is too liable to perversion that can seriously impede the proper functioning of the economy.

3. That business confidence can be fostered by "taxing diffidence" is, to say the least, highly doubtful.

4. Subsidies for some business are likely to be at the expense of other business—a process resulting in much unfairness and no net gain in initiative.

An economy run by its tax system is indeed the tail wagging the dog!

Morale is a large factor in business motivation, and morale is supported by a sense of fair play and stability in government-business relations. Furthermore, the quantity and particularly the quality of governmental expenditures have a bearing on economic incentives. These are large and engaging subjects, but they cannot be covered in this report.

3. BACKGROUND OF THE FEDERAL TAX PROBLEM

During much of our history, the federal government relied principally on tariffs and excises to provide its revenue. Income and inheritance taxes were not introduced until shortly before our entrance into the First World War. These taxes, at first very moderately employed, were pushed into high gear to finance the war. To them were added the excess-profits taxes. These business taxes—the corporate income and excess-profits tax—produced what was then regarded as extremely high financial returns to the government, 3.16

[1] Such as reestablishment of balanced international trade and financial relations; agricultural adjustment, both to the domestic and to the world situation; relations of labor and management; maintenance of an effective balance between consumption and productive capacity; and the effective cooperation between government and industry. (This list was suggested in Harold G. Moulton and Karl Schlotterbeck, *Collapse or Boom at the End of the War*, The Brookings Institution, Washington, D.C., 1942.)

billion dollars in 1918. After the war the excess-profits tax was repealed; and during the twenties the personal income-tax rates were, in successive acts, substantially reduced. In spite of these reductions, a balanced budget was maintained, and the debt was cut more than a third.

The financial upheaval of the thirties brought increased tax rates, but revenues did not increase sufficiently to balance the budget. New taxes included an excess-profits capital-stock tax on corporations. This was based on the declared value of capital stock and amounted to an additional levy on net income, "estimated" in advance. An undistributed-profits tax was introduced in 1936 but was greatly reduced in 1938 and abandoned in 1939. Pay roll taxes to finance social security were initiated in 1935.

As the system stood in 1939, the personal income tax carried a personal exemption of $2500 for a married couple, a normal rate of 4 per cent, and a maximum surtax rate of 75 per cent on income in excess of $5,000,000. The corporation rate was graduated from 12½ to 19 per cent. Together these two taxes produced about 40 per cent of federal revenue. Consumption taxes (mainly excises on liquor and tobacco) continued to occupy an important place, supplying 29 per cent of the revenue. More was collected from liquor and tobacco taxes than from the personal income tax! Pay roll taxes added 14 per cent to the revenue. Import tariffs had faded to an inconsequential fiscal role; and the estates tax, with a high top rate of 70 per cent, was also relatively insignificant as a revenue producer.

The present war has brought tax increases all along the line. Personal exemptions in the personal income tax have been substantially reduced (from $2500 to $1200 for a married couple), and the number of income-tax payers has increased from 4 to about 50 millions. Bottom rates on taxable income have risen to about 22 per cent compared with 4 per cent in 1939, and top rates range to about 90 per cent on income in excess of $200,000. Business taxes mount to a top corporation normal and surtax of 40 per cent in addition to an excess-profits tax of 95 per cent. Neither business tax is deductible in calculating the other, but excess-profits net income is not subject to the corporation tax, an over-all limitation of 80 per cent is allowed, and 10 per cent of excess-profits taxes is ear-

TABLE I

ESTIMATED ANNUAL REVENUE YIELD OF FEDERAL TAXES UNDER THE 1944 ACT
AT 1944 LEVEL OF INCOME *

(In millions of dollars)

Taxes	Estimated Revenue	
Corporation taxes:		
Capital stock...............................	$ 400.0	
Declared-value excess profits.....................	104.7	
Excess profits................................	10,042.5	
Income.......................................	4,819.2	
Total......................................		$15,366.4
Personal taxes:		
Income.......................................	$17,955.8†	
Estate..	522.4	
Gift..	40.2	
Total......................................		18,518.4
Social-security taxes:		
Total employment taxes.........................	$ 2,160.3	2,160.3
Other taxes:		
Customs......................................	$ 400.0	
Excises—commodities and services................	5,094.0	
Miscellaneous.................................	1,124.2	
Total......................................		6,618.2
Grand total.................................		$42,663.3

* Source: "Revenue Revision of 1943," *House Ways and Means Committee Hearings*, pp. 53–55. As modified by treasury estimates of changes resulting from the 1944 act.

† Some portion of this sum, possibly 1.5 billion dollars, will be due to overlapping collections from the 1942 and 1943 incomes.

marked as a postwar credit. The excess-profits tax is levied on the excess of current profits over prewar earnings or a percentage return on capital, whichever is higher. Out of 42 billion dollars of estimated revenue for a full year's operation of the present federal tax system,[1] the corporate-profits and income taxes will produce some 15 billion dollars and the

[1] See Table I.

personal income tax some 18 billion dollars (including 1.5 billion attributable to overlapping payments attending the introduction of more current collection).

So much by way of a brief introduction to our subject. The following chapters seek to outline ways and means for recasting the postwar federal revenue system in the interest of high production and employment. No attempt is made to cover all elements in the federal tax system or all problems of federal taxation. The discussion is confined to major issues involved in the problem here singled out for attention.

III. INTEGRATION OF CORPORATE AND PERSONAL TAXES

1. HISTORICAL SURVEY

THE first federal income tax, introduced in 1913, used the corporation income tax chiefly as a withholding levy. The rate of tax on corporate income was the same as the normal rate of the personal income tax. Dividends were exempted from the normal personal tax. Thus double taxation was avoided. This policy continued through the First World War, although both the normal and the corporate rates were raised to 12 per cent during this period. In the early twenties the relationship between the two taxes was broken when the corporate rate was raised to 12½ per cent and later to still higher figures, while the normal personal tax was reduced to 8 per cent and subsequently to lower levels. In 1936, when dividends were made subject to the normal tax, the divorce between the two levies was completed. What had once been a withholding levy was thus converted into a full-fledged business tax. Both before and during the Second World War the trend in federal taxation has been to rely heavily on taxation of business as such.

2. CRITICAL ANALYSIS OF THE PRESENT SYSTEM AND TREND

The following analysis leads to the conclusion that the duplication in the corporate and personal income taxes should be eliminated by integrating the two levies.

A. The "Theoretical" Basis of a Business Tax, While Plausible, Is Inconclusive

A plausible case for business taxes is made by public-finance writers who point out that these taxes are an appropriate return for benefits received by corporations from government

and for the special privileges that corporations enjoy. Moreover, they argue that corporations have ability to pay quite
apart from that of their stockholders and that business taxation
affords a needed instrument of social control. "The strictly
personal or individual concept of ability to pay must be supple-
mented by an impersonal or group concept of it." It is also
pointed out that no direct relation exists between the volume
of business and the value of property employed; there may be
much property with little business, and vice versa. Accordingly, business taxes based on volume are said to be needed to
supplement the property tax.[1] These views are not accepted
by all public-finance writers. Some of them are unable to
make any sense out of the corporate levy and see in the combination of a federal corporate income tax and the taxation
of dividends to stockholders a clear case of duplication, confusion, and discrimination.[2]

In the author's view, such a "theoretical" approach in
terms of benefits, privileges, and abilities provides no definitive
answer to the question: Should business as such be taxed?
*The real answer must be sought by analyzing the effects and incidence
of business taxes.*

Most of the benefits of government are provided in the
common interest and are not subject to apportionment. The
benefit theory offers support for taxation in general, but it
provides no satisfactory clue as to how taxes should be distributed. Relevant here is the conclusion of E. R. A. Seligman[3] that taxes are "compulsory contributions to defray the
expenses incurred in the common interest, without any reference to particular advantages accruing to the taxpayer."

[1] See T. S. Adams, "The Taxation of Business," *Proceedings of the National Tax Association*, 1917, pp. 185–194; Gerhard Colm, "Conflicting Theories of Corporate Income Taxation," *Law and Contemporary Problems*, Duke University, pp. 281–290; 1940, Paul Studenski, "Toward a Theory of Business Taxation," *Journal of Political Economy*, Vol. XLVIII, No. 5, 1940, pp. 621–654.

[2] Roswell Magill, *The Impact of Federal Taxes*, Columbia University Press, New York, 1943.

[3] E. R. A. Seligman, *Essays in Taxation*, 10th ed., The Macmillan Company, New York, 1925, p. 415.

Certainly business would not get far in the anarchy that would prevail without government, but neither would the wage earner, professional man, or any other citizen. There are cases of *special* benefit, to be sure, but these are usually financed by special assessments. In general, however, there is no calculus by which to determine what proportion of either the cost or the benefit of government can be justly attributed to each taxpayer. It is impossible to say in what degree various taxpayers benefit from a battleship.

In the last analysis, all taxes come out of the income or capital (actual or potential) of *individuals*. Tax burdens cannot be borne by inanimate objects. Will division among individuals be more equitable or otherwise more desirable if business taxes are levied? This is the important question, and in searching for the answer one gets little guidance from a consideration of benefits.

Specific schemes of business taxation based upon the benefit theory are usually vulnerable to attack on the score that they involve arbitrary classification. The corporate net income tax takes no account of the fact that corporations enjoy the favorable environment created by government whether or not they show a net profit. A gross income tax would therefore seem to be more in harmony with the theory. But a gross income tax encounters a multitude of variables among corporations, and many of these variables would have a bearing on benefit accounting. A business levy confined to corporations can hardly be supported in the name of benefits; yet if the tax is broadened to cover all business, how shall "business" be defined? Shall it include farmers? Professional people? Wage earners? "Coupon-clippers"? For all the guidance we get from the benefit theory, we might resolve the problem by taxing all individuals twice on their personal income, once for the benefits enjoyed in production and once for benefits enjoyed as consumers.

It is not at all clear that we *should* distribute federal taxes according to benefits even if we *could*. A case can be made for pricing governmental services according to the income level of the beneficiary rather than according to the value of the service. The benefit theory is widely applied and firmly entrenched in the tax systems of state and local governments, where circumstances allow less choice than that enjoyed by the federal government. (The latter has greater power to borrow, is free from threats of taxpayer migration, and need have no fear of unequal competition.) The federal government might well reject this method of tax apportionment even if it had a feasible means of applying it.

Corporations do receive a special privilege in the grant of the right to operate as limited-liability associations. This is the basis of many franchise taxes that now confuse and complicate the tax systems of many units of government. Under modern general incorporation laws, however, this privilege is available for the asking. If competition were effective, the value of this privilege would be reduced to zero. It is true that competition is not that efficient, but corporation taxes make no pretense of measuring the results of monopolistic practices. Granted that there is some value to the privilege of incorporation, what this value is in any given case is entirely a matter of guesswork. Moreover, the states, not the federal government, grant most corporation franchises.

It is plausibly contended that business entities have ability to pay independent of that of their stockholders. Businesses do have one important ability in this respect, namely, the power to meet tax bills. And businesses undoubtedly differ among themselves in this regard. But again the weakness in this approach is apparent when specific application is attempted. For example, if ability to pay is to serve as the basis of a corporate income tax, can the ratio of earnings to capital invested be ignored? If the answer is negative, we are plunged into the realm of excess-profits taxation. Then the question arises: Can we accept the ratio of income to capital as a measure of ability without attention to the varying degree of risk involved in producing the income? Confronted by the obvious impracticability of making due allowance for risk, we return to the question of whether, since all taxes are finally borne by individuals, we gain anything from the standpoint of ability to pay by levying on individuals indirectly through business taxes.

Extended consideration cannot be given here to the use of business taxes for social control. The graduated corporation tax may, through its differentials, aid small business. Because of their place in the life of small communities and because of their possible value as a check upon monopoly, small companies have a claim for special consideration. However, small business should not be confused with new business or with competitive business, either of which may be a more suitable object of social concern. Moreover, the graduated corporation tax aids not only small business but also large business with a small income. The tax on intercorporate dividends discourages holding companies and intercorporate investment, but it fails to distinguish between "good" and "bad" holding companies. And there are, of course, other ways of aiding small business and policing holding companies. Corporate taxation has been supported on the ground that it checks concentration of control by preventing corporations from becoming too large; but there is no convincing evidence that the tax has been at all successful in this role. The conclusion is that taxation of corporate income is not sufficiently discriminating or otherwise valuable for social control to warrant its retention on this ground alone.

B. *Incidence of the Corporate Income Tax*

The view that the incidence, or final burden, of the corporate income tax falls on the stockholders is widely held and is claimed to be in accord with the dictates of common sense. But many businessmen and a considerable number of theorists disagree, holding that the tax is shifted, at least in part, and that a reduction in the tax would mean a fall in prices. A few go so far as to call the levy a sales tax in disguise. Others hold that wages are also affected by the tax. No useful purpose would be served by reviewing either the intricate theory involved in dealing with this question of incidence or the "polls of opinion" that have been taken concerning the proper answer.[1] Suffice it to say that no certain conclusion is possible and that not improbably the burden is divided at least between stockholders and consumers.

One of the weakest spots in the armor of business taxes is the obscurity of their incidence. This is less true of the corporate net income tax than of other business levies; but, as already explained, there is much doubt as to the ultimate distribution of burden even in the case of levies on net business income. When the ultimate bearers of the burden and the degree of their participation are uncertain, it is hardly possible to appraise a tax. If neither the benefits for which compensation is sought nor the ultimate burden of the tax is discernible, the principal characteristic of the levy would seem to be the thick cloud of confusion that hangs over it.

The incidence of the corporate income tax is either on the stockholders or on some other element involved in the economic process, possibly wage earners, though more probably consumers. If it falls on wage earners or consumers, there can be no particular logic or equity in the tax, and "happenstance" will determine the division. If the burden is on the stockholders, not only are they being taxed twice, but the division among them is certain to be prejudicial to small stockholders. An impersonal tax takes no account of the circumstances of the stockholders. The fallacy of the corporation tax arises from treating corporations as though they were persons and as though it were possible for business entities to bear a tax in their own right.

[1] See National Industrial Conference Board, *The Shifting and Effects of the Federal Corporation Income Tax*, Vol. I, 1928; *Report of the Committee on National Debt and Taxation*, London, 1927; E. R. A. Seligman, "Income Taxes and the Price Level," *Academy of Political Science Proceedings*, Vol. XI, 1924, pp. 3–23; Dennis H. Robertson, *Economic Fragments*, P. S. King & Son, Ltd., London, 1931, pp. 23–41.

C. *Effects of the Corporate Tax upon Incentives*

As previously stated, the common conclusion that the corporate tax is borne by the stockholders involves the corollary that two income taxes are imposed on the profit element in income, whereas only one is imposed on most other income. The use of a corporate tax along with the full personal tax on dividends puts a special penalty upon risk-taking. The results of this double burden at present top rates and at the margin of income can be seen in Table II.

TABLE II

THE EFFECT ON INVESTMENT YIELDS OF A PROFITS TAX OF 80 PER CENT AND A PERSONAL INCOME TAX OF 90 PER CENT AT THEIR MAXIMUM EFFECTIVENESS*
(Yield expressed as per cent of corporate investment)

Corporate-profits yield before taxes	Corporate-profits yield after corporate taxes	Net yield to individual after individual taxes
10	2	0.2
25	5	0.5
50	10	1.0
100	20	2.0
200	40	4.0

* Rates assumed are approximately the maximum provided in the present federal law.

There is reason to believe that decisions concerning production and expansion are influenced more by management's interest in the company's earning record than by hope of a high return for investors. Managers are extremely and sometimes irrationally interested in the growth of their companies, and much of the satisfaction derived from business activity is linked to the standing of the company and not to the size of the return to stockholders. To relieve the tax system of repressive effects, first attention should go to the active businessman as such; less concern is required for the passive investor. Of course, businesses must have capital, and venturesome enterprises will encounter a scarcity of funds if the rewards to investors are too limited. But management can often get the means as well as the incentive to expand from the earnings of the business unit. The company's success, with which management identifies personal success, is measured first by corporate net earnings, next by dividends, and least by dividends net of personal tax.

If business taxes do reduce investment, employment, and national income, and other taxes can be found that would not do this, then the price we pay for business taxes is too high. Their elimination would mean higher personal incomes, a larger tax base, and greater general welfare.

D. Bond versus Stock Financing

The duplication of taxes, previously discussed, applies only to investment in stocks. A dollar of income that is earmarked for the bondholder is paid to him in full, but the profit dollar that is earmarked for the stockholder is, in effect, cut to 60 cents. This encourages corporations to issue bonds instead of stock.

That the present discrimination is substantial and that it does exercise an unfortunate influence upon corporate and individual decisions in many cases is confirmed by accountants and others close to corporate financing. Obviously if a company pays out to bondholders half its net income (before federal taxes and the payment of interest), it can save half the corporate tax that would be due were the company to finance itself exclusively with stock. The higher the effective rate of the corporation tax, the greater the saving. With a 40 per cent effective tax rate and average earnings of 5 per cent on capital and with a distribution of half of net operating income to bondholders, the saving would amount to 1 per cent on the capital (5 per cent $\times$ 50 per cent $\times$ 40 per cent = 1 per cent).

The undesirable effects of excessive bond financing have been described as follows:[1]

Heavy fixed (or floating) debt is obviously undesirable for the single enterprise in an unstable economy or industry. Any tempo-

[1] Henry C. Simons, memorandum submitted to the author.

rary adversity is likely to produce insolvency, with grave losses, not only for the stockholders but also for senior securities and the enterprise as a whole, through the great costs of reorganization and the inevitable disturbances of operations and business relations which insolvency involves. Moreover, even if technical insolvency and reorganization are avoided, the enterprise and the whole economy may gravely be damaged by the practices necessary in avoiding it. Thus, physical properties may be abused merely to prolong technical, legal solvency, to avoid definitive squeezing out of shareholders, management, or "control" in bankruptcy or reorganization, and thus to gamble (with nothing to lose!) on remotely favorable contingencies. The physical plant may thus be "bled white" to meet current obligations, especially interest payment and bond maturities, in the pursuit of mere liquidity.

These things are doubtless widely understood. What is less clearly apprehended is the aggravated instability of the whole economy, and the obstacle to deliberate monetary stabilization, which corporate debt structures produce in their aggregate. It should be obvious what desperate and frantic struggles for corporate liquidity mean in total where the economy has slipped into general recession which, debt structures apart, might prove innocuous and short-lived. They may well mean the difference between a mild recession and a precipitous, catastrophic deflation.

There is wide support for the view that it is undesirable to use the credit relationship in business transactions otherwise than to facilitate current operations. According to this view, business should operate without long-term dollar contracts and avoid the dangers of insolvency and speculation in the value of money that such contracts entail.

The Securities and Exchange Commission and state utility commissions call constantly for a reduction in bonded debt, but they are shouted down by a tax system that has exactly the opposite bias.

The discrimination that favors bond financing could be removed by taxing the operating income of corporations (including the bond interest) instead of the net income. This alleged solution is supported by many competent critics, who maintain that the distinction between stock and debtor capital is not one that should be recognized by the tax system. In the development of the large, quasi-public corporation, it is said, the distinction between creditors and stockholders has become blurred and that between bondholders and preferred stockholders has largely disappeared. However, a tax on net operating income could and would force some concerns into bankruptcy. On the other hand, since part of the income tax would fall on an element of cost as distinguished from final profit, part of the tax would be more easily shifted to the consumer. Moreover, if net operating income were to become the base of the tax, should not rent paid as well as interest paid be disallowed as a deduction? And why stop with rent paid? Why not disallow the deduction of all expenses and have a gross income tax?

Another objection to the taxation of operating income is that the transition to such a basis would involve many difficulties. Since much financing is on a long-term basis, this transition would need to be gradual, and even then adjustments might prove very disturbing to the finance and business structure.

A more sensible approach to the problem of eliminating the discrimination between stock and bond financing would be to move in the opposite direction—that is, to allow a credit against either the corporation or the personal tax for the element of duplication. This would mean that, whether the corporation were financed with stocks or bonds, its earnings would be subject to only one tax.

E. Equity of the Corporate Tax

It has been shown that the duplication of personal and corporate taxes rests with special weight upon the profit element in income. Since profits tend to be concentrated in the higher income brackets, the steeply graduated personal tax places an average tax burden on profits in excess of that on other income elements. This is justified as a necessary antidote for concentration in income distribution, but questions may be raised as to whether the progression should be compounded by doubling up the corporation and individual taxes.

The corporation income tax is as unsatisfactory to those whose principal interest is in the fairness of the tax system as to those whose principal concern is for incentives. As we have seen, an unknown but probably considerable part of this tax becomes an element in prices and is paid by consumers in haphazard amounts and proportions. Moreover, the tax is necessarily impersonal in character and makes no differentiation among stockholders according to income status. The small stockholder, sometimes mainly dependent upon a small income from stocks, is subjected to the same treatment as the wealthy investor. Extractions from income at the level of corporate earnings cannot again appear in the base of the personal tax. It would be better for all concerned were all income to run the gantlet of the tax system only once and at the personal level. Here it could be taxed as severely as the needs of the government and the interest in equalizing the distribution of income might require.

Some justification for corporate income taxation might be based on the fact that corporations often reinvest a considerable portion of their earnings and that this income might escape the tax system entirely were it not for the corporation tax. The problem of taxing undistributed earnings under the income tax, one of the most difficult in the field of taxation, will be considered shortly. It should be observed, however, that the present system, levying two taxes on the distributed portion of earnings and one undifferentiated impersonal tax on the undistributed portion, is an exceedingly crude and unsatisfactory solution of the problem.

F. Other Considerations

Business taxation has had perhaps its strongest support on the score that it is necessary in order to raise adequate revenue. This point will be examined in more detail later. The fiscal necessity of business taxes is not at all established. In spite of heavy governmental costs, the British managed without an independent business tax until 1937 and employed it thereafter only at the nominal rate of 5 per cent.

Duplication of corporate and personal taxes at the state level (where it often but by no means universally occurs) is less difficult to defend than that at the federal level. In state tax systems, the corporate levy reaches the net income of absentee investors, and the inclusion of dividends in the individual tax bases is necessary for the fair application of the personal tax. Even here, however, a credit for corporation taxes could and should be allowed in the state where dividends are received.

These considerations lead to the conclusion that corporate and personal taxes should be entirely (or at least largely) integrated. No prospective modification of the tax system rests on firmer ground, and none is more important. Integration of corporate and personal taxes can be viewed as the elimination of the corporate levy, but it also constitutes a very substantial reduction in the personal income tax. The theoretical basis of a business tax, while plausible, is inconclusive; its incidence is uncertain and confusing; and its effects are unduly repressive and discriminatory. The strongest case for the tax rests on the ground that it yields well and that certain possible substitutes are worse. But this is hardly sufficient justification for its use, especially since there are acceptable alternatives that can supply the required revenue. It must be recognized, however, that any integration program runs head on into the tax treatment of undistributed profits, a problem to which we now turn our attention.

3. UNDISTRIBUTED PROFITS
A. Cause for Action—Discrimination

Disinterested critics are generally agreed that the present tax treatment of undistributed corporate earnings is unsatisfactory. The present system applies two taxes to income that passes through the corporation and one to income that is reinvested by the company. It allows an individual to become indefinitely rich for an indefinite period without paying any personal income tax. To be sure, the tax system may "catch up" with such an individual through the taxation of realized capital gains or through application of the death tax to his estate, but the realization of capital gains can be postponed as long as stock continues to be owned by the same stockholder. It may be further postponed as long as the stock is retained by the heirs of the original owner or the heirs of the heirs, and so on.[1] The death tax is only a delayed and partial compensation for privileges enjoyed in the application of the tax system during the life of the deceased. Thus a strong case in terms of equity can be made for a relatively more rigorous application of the tax system to undistributed profits. In addition, the apparent necessity for at least one levy on undistributed earnings has been used to justify the unfortunate duplication of corporate and personal levies.

B. *Cause for Action—Avoidance*

The present treatment of undistributed corporate income is also objectionable on the ground that it is an open invitation to tax avoidance. Why should corporations declare dividends beyond the consumption needs of their stockholders, when to do so involves much heavier taxes than if management were to do the investing for them?

Various devices have been introduced into the tax laws to check this obvious leakage. Since the inauguration of the federal tax, the possibility of using a corporation as a "savings bank" to avoid personal income surtaxes has been recognized. Special taxes have been designed to prevent this practice.

---

[1] Moreover, as the law is at present applied, the basis for the gain in the hands of an heir is not the basis of the decedent; nor is the basis for a donee necessarily that of the donor. In the first case, the value at the time of the death transfer serves as the new basis; in the latter case, the basis used is that in the hands of the donor in the case of a gain and the donor's basis or the value at the time of the transfer, whichever is lower, in the case of a loss.

The acts that were passed prior to 1921 did not attempt to attack the problem through the corporation itself but rather chose to strike directly at the stockholders. This they did by taxing the stockholders (of companies improperly accumulating surplus) on their respective prorata shares of the corporation's earnings. In 1920, however, the Supreme Court decision in *Eisner v. Macomber*[1] raised some doubt as to the constitutionality of this method. The 1921 Act and subsequent acts have imposed "penalty" tax rates for improper accumulation directly on the corporation.

The problem of protecting the revenue without thwarting legitimate corporate expansion is a delicate one. Section 102 of the revenue laws, considerably strengthened by the 1938 Act, makes accumulation of surplus beyond the reasonable needs of the business the equivalent of tax avoidance unless the corporation, by a clear preponderance of the evidence, proves the contrary. Investment in assets having no reasonable connection with the business is usually ground for applying Section 102 of the law. But it is generally recognized that this feature of the revenue laws is feeble.[2] Corporate reinvestment is typically the result of mixed motives, and a plausible defense for it is usually not very difficult to discover. Logically, avoidance attends all corporate reinvestment regardless of how legitimate it may be. From the point of view of all parties concerned, the uncertainties connected with this whole procedure are thoroughly bad. Moreover, the administration of Section 102 may interfere with legitimate attempts to develop liquid corporate reserves.[3]

[1] 252 U.S. 189 (1920).

[2] The reaction of one competent critic to the experience with this feature of the law is as follows: "Through most of our history this approach has just been a farce and beginning in 1938 it began to be an unmitigated nuisance." At one time the Packard Motor Company had a $14,400,000 investment in government bonds. There was nothing improper in this, and the liquid reserve enabled the company to weather adversity and to maintain its financial and operating strength while shifting production to low-priced cars.

[3] The attempt to apply penalty rates of tax is irrational and oppressive on small stockholders. The procedure followed before 1921 was much better and

Another means of preventing improper accumulation of reinvested funds is to create a separate tax classification for companies designated as "personal holding companies." This was begun in 1934 and has been continued in later acts. The classification includes closely held companies engaged very largely in the investment business. The concerns so classed are subject to a special and severe corporation tax. In contrast with Section 102, liability in the case of this special type of company is a matter of objective facts and not one of motivation. Early laws contained loopholes, such as the exclusion of rent, in determining the portion of the business to be classed as "investment." These were plugged in later legislation. However, the line between "personal holding companies" and "near-personal holding companies" is necessarily arbitrary. A great improvement in this field (applying to both holding companies and those subject to Section 102 penalties) could be made by requiring the stockholders of these companies to be taxed (as is now the case with foreign personal holding companies) on their prorata share of undistributed income. This would avoid pressure to distribute earnings and would apply tax burdens most equitably among stockholders. The option of using the prorata method should be open to all concerns at all times.

C. *Social and Economic Effects of Corporate Saving*

The social and economic effects of corporate saving is a broad subject and one that gives rise to controversy at many points. Only a brief inquiry into some of the issues involved

---

that of Canada still better. The Canadian system provides that if, in the judgment of the Minister of National Revenue, the accumulation is unreasonable, he may notify the corporation to that effect and may designate the amount which he deems excessive. If this amount is not distributed during the year in which the notice is given, the shareholders are presumed to have received it as a dividend on the last day of the tax year and are taxed accordingly.

Harry J. Rudick, "Section 102 and the Personal Holding Company Provisions of the Internal Revenue Code," *Yale Law Journal*, Vol. XLIX, p. 171, 1939.

See also *Canadian Income War Tax Act*, Part IV, Chap. 97, Sec. 13, Revised Statutes, 1927.

can be attempted here. There is a difference of opinion among students of corporation finance as to whether the present power of management to invest corporate earnings, subject to a relatively weak indirect control of the stockholder, is in the social interest. Those opposed to corporate reinvestment of earnings argue that the temptation for management to gain power and prestige with other people's money is very strong and that the present system is not conducive to the best allocation of resources. Reinvestment enables the firm to avoid exposing its plans to the test of the market. In reply, it has been pointed out that many investors give inadequate weight in their decisions to the long-run interests of their company and, particularly, that they underrate the reserves needed for business stability. Some contend that corporate savings aggravate a tendency toward overexpansion of productive equipment and that this creates depressions. The answer offered to this is that even more investment is needed in order to provide full employment. In addition, it is said that reserves mitigate the business cycle because they enable corporations to continue payments for wages, materials, taxes, and so forth, during bad times.

The proponents of corporate savings emphasize that this source of capital constitutes an important means of business expansion and diversification and that its favorable treatment would encourage risk capital. This favorable treatment is particularly important in the case of small and new companies, for which the capital market may be prohibitively expensive. About half of new equity capital in recent years has come from reinvestment.

It is fairly well agreed that corporate savings for business (not tax-evasion) purposes serve a useful function and that they should not be discouraged by the tax system. To say that they warrant preferred tax treatment is, however, another matter. Except for new enterprises of small size, where access to capital is known to be limited, corporate savings would seem to have no convincing claim to preference over savings by unincorporated companies and individuals. While occasionally it is suggested that all savings should be given preferred treatment in the income-tax system, the exemption of savings from the personal income-tax base has never been seriously entertained either in the United States or elsewhere. Certainly any program of this sort would be a far cry from the underinvestment-oversaving theories that have in recent years gained considerable acceptance in respectable circles. In these quarters a special tax on savings was sought to prod them into activity. If it were thought desirable to differentiate between savings and investment on the part of a business concern, corporate saving which is converted into plant and equipment (and which thus provides employment) might be given preferred treatment over that which is held in cash or other liquid assets. Yet some liquid reserves are admittedly desirable as a contributing factor to business stability. On the whole, equal treatment for all income whether saved or invested, and whether the disposition is by corporations or by others, would appear to be the safest rule.

D. Historical Survey

For many years business leaders have been told that they would be well advised to accept an undistributed-profits tax in lieu of the duplication in corporate and individual levies and as more desirable than excess-profits taxation. After the First World War, the undistributed-profits tax was proposed as a fitting substitute for the excess-profits tax. However, the excess-profits tax was abandoned, not in favor of the undistributed-profits tax, but in favor of duplication in the corporate and personal levies.

In 1936 an undistributed-profits tax was brought into the federal tax system. The measure passed by Congress rejected the original program of the administration and substituted a hastily devised makeshift. The duplication in the corporate and personal levies was retained. Adding the undistributed-profits tax resulted in a triple burden on business earnings—one upon corporate income, one upon undistributed income, and one upon any ultimate distribution of the income currently reinvested or upon the capital gains of the stockholder when he disposed of his stock at a profit. The undistributed-profits tax was criticized as interfering with the freedom of management to make decisions concerning expansion entirely on business considerations. It was claimed further that the tax created undue hardship in obtaining capital and thus discouraged investment and that it was particularly prejudicial to small and growing companies, which encounter difficulties in recruiting new capital in the open market. The failure to provide for a carry-over of losses added greatly to the hardship. The tax was vigorously opposed and much resented by the business world. As previously remarked, managers have a high regard for the growth of their companies. What the growth glands are to the human body, undistributed profits are to a business. The tax was reduced in 1938 and repealed in 1939. But the problem that it sought to solve still remains.

E. *Alternative Remedies*

Many modifications of the present treatment of undistributed earnings and the duplication of corporate and individual taxes have been proposed. Three of the most promising will be considered.

1. *Treating Corporations like Partnerships*

One solution to the problem of taxing undistributed earnings would require the paper distribution of such income or the assessment of stockholders upon their prorata shares of reinvested earnings. This has strong claim to support from the standpoint of equity. It would apply "proper" taxes to corporate saving without subsidy or penalty. It would free management from pressure to modify any dividend policy that seemed desirable from the standpoint of business needs alone. Corporations would be treated for tax purposes like associations of individuals, as is now the case with partnerships. This procedure has precedent in our Civil War income tax. In recent years it has also been applied quite extensively to foreign personal holding companies and personal service corporations. However, the procedure involves administrative difficulties, especially in applying it to large corporations, and (as explained below) it jolts the popular conception of the relation of the corporation to the stockholder.

The legal feasibility of the partnership method in treating undistributed corporate income is open to some question, but there are probably no insuperable legal barriers to this solution of the problem. For forty years or more, courts have pointed out repeatedly that for certain purposes the corporate entity must be disregarded in order to deal with the rights and responsibilities of the real persons involved. In the field of taxation, with which we are concerned, there has been a frequent shuffling back and forth in this matter from one position to the other. Persistent efforts to tax stock dividends as income are one symptom of the tendency to minimize the concept of a distinct corporate institution. The *Eisner v. Macomber* decision[1] stands for the separate-entity view; but it was made over the protest of a strong dissent, and the Supreme Court may be in a receptive mood for an invitation to knock down this landmark.

The administrative difficulties involved in the proposal to treat corporations like partnerships for taxation purposes are formidable; but these, too, have been exaggerated by some critics. It must not be forgotten that of the 400,000 to 500,000 corporations, only a few thousand are large institutions with long lists of stockholders scattered over the country. For smaller companies, the partnership method of taxation would present no very great administrative difficulties. For companies with complicated financial structures, it might be difficult to determine how the undistributed profits should be allocated among various classes of stockholders for tax pur-

[1] 252 U.S. 189 (1920).

poses, and it would be particularly difficult where several holding companies lay between the operating corporation and the individual stockholder.[1] Moreover, reinvestment currently taxed should not be taxed again as capital gains. This would require either elimination of capital gains and losses on stocks from the tax base or a complicated adjustment to compensate for accumulated changes in surplus. Some embarrassment would be caused if corporations were field-audited some years after a report of income and a substantial change in the taxable corporate incomes were to result. Adjustments would be necessary in the income-tax bases of all the stockholders, numbering, in the case of some single corporations, tens or hundreds of thousands. But this hazard would be confined mainly to large corporations and might be minimized (perhaps constitutionally) by altering taxpayers' current income rather than reopening past returns.

Far more significant as objections to the partnership method are the psychological and political impediments. The taxation of corporations as partnerships violates the popular conceptions of income and of the relation of stockholders to corporations. Through decades of custom, corporations have come to be considered as institutions apart from their stockholders, and the income of the former is not regarded as belonging to the latter until dividends are declared.

Closely related to this point is the contention that stockholders would incur a hardship if they were taxed upon what they had not actually received. Corporations might overcome this to some extent by distributing cash or stock dividends to meet the stockholders' tax liability; but the fact remains that the requirements of the stockholder, and particularly the minority stockholder, are often not very articulate in corporate

---

[1] Actually, under modern corporation law, at least in some states, the right of the stockholder to a fixed place in the capital structure is not absolute, and a pattern of hypothetical distribution, once announced, might not be followed at a later time. (See Adolf Berle and Gardiner C. Means, *The Modern Corporation and Private Property*, The Macmillan Company, New York, 1933, pp. 148–151.)

policy. The small stockholder is likely to feel that a bird in the corporation bush is far from a bird in his own hand.[1]

It should not be too difficult to convince the owners of thousands of small companies (which are often little more than incorporated partnerships or family groups) that a tax system which treated their companies like partnerships would be a great improvement over the present duplication of personal and corporate levies. Owners of the larger corporations would be more difficult to convince, and they would have more valid grounds for their objections. The situation might warrant a classification according to size, with small companies being treated like partnerships and large ones paying a compensatory undistributed-profits tax, adjusted as nearly as feasible to exact from the corporation the equivalent of what stockholders would pay were all earnings distributed. But the compensatory undistributed-profits tax would not be a very satisfactory means of tax integration, and the chances are that it would incur the same political hostility heaped upon the

[1] It is true that corporations can distribute taxable stock dividends or other taxable securities to make a division of earnings while retaining their profits for reinvestment. This makes it possible for a corporation to have its cake and eat it, too, so to speak. But this procedure also has difficulties and limitations. "Capital structures of corporations should not be controlled by tax avoidance considerations." At present, stock dividends are not income to the recipient as long as they do not disturb proportionate equities in the company. The use of stock dividends for tax purposes as a paper distribution of taxable profits would be facilitated if the Supreme Court were to modify its rule that common stock dividends issued to common stockholders are not income. There is a strong possibility that the Supreme Court might do this were Congress to express a clear preference for this interpretation. But a stock dividend is much more than a paper distribution of earnings. It involves a commitment as to the ultimate distribution of, and responsibility for, capital which goes considerably beyond the mere building up of surplus. Stock dividends are hardly an available instrument for a concern with an accumulated deficit from past operations. Moreover, they would be inconvenient as a paper distribution of small reinvestments. Finally, they involve difficult problems of valuation. Should the value accepted for tax purposes be the proportionate share of earnings presently added to surplus or the market value of stocks distributed? The last word on the instrumentation of paper distribution of reinvested earnings has not been written, but until better techniques are available it must be concluded that the use of this device does not provide an adequate solution of the problems of partnership procedure.

"noble experiment" of 1936. If undistributed earnings are to receive any favors, they should be the earnings of new small companies especially dependent upon this source for new equity capital.

In the political environment that followed the twenties, when the emphasis was placed on the dangers of overexpansion, a solution along the lines just discussed might have had a chance for acceptance. In the political environment that will follow the war, with its probable emphasis upon expansion and growth of industry, a solution of this kind is not likely to be greeted with enthusiasm.

Nevertheless, the partnership method, with or without classification, does have merit, and it might well be considered in seeking a solution of the integration problem after the war. It is the most logical, direct, and uncompromising solution of this difficult issue. Certainly, it should be applied to all personal holding companies and corporations already subject to special laws for improper accumulation. And other corporations, with appropriate limitations, might be permitted to use the system at their option.

2. *Taxing Undistributed Earnings Only through Rigorous Taxation of Capital Gains*

It has been suggested that the corporate tax be abandoned entirely and that the capital-gains tax be relied upon to reach undistributed corporate earnings. This means taxing at the full personal rate any increase in the value of a security at the time of its sale or transfer.

At present, undistributed profits are taxed once to the corporation through the general corporate income tax and once to the stockholder through the personal tax when capital gains are realized. However, the personal tax does not apply fully to capital gains. To make the capital-gains tax fully effective the following changes would be required: ceiling rate and other special rate provisions would have to be removed; limitations on deductions of capital losses would have to be lifted; gains and losses on transfer by gift and at the death of the taxpayer would have to be made taxable. Were the corporation tax removed from the picture and capital gains made fully taxable, undistributed earnings would eventually be subject to the personal tax completely and to it only.

The capital-gains tax, as a means of applying the personal tax to undistributed corporate income, would favor the retention of earnings in the corporation because of the postponement of the tax. The taxpayer would also have some choice as to the time when his share of reinvested earnings would be realized. Reinvestments offset by losses would be fully canceled. These advantages would undoubtedly be very stimulating to corporate saving and reinvestment. One proponent[1] describes the system as saying to the owner of corporation stock, in effect,

Leave your earnings in the business if you so desire. I won't tax you, while you live, on any earnings reinvested. In fairness to other taxpayers, you and I must have a final and comprehensive reckoning sometime (after you are gone or, if you get indolent with age, when you retire from ownership participation in the enterprise). Pending that time, however, you may, as it were, borrow from me without interest what you would pay additionally under partnership procedure. . . . Besides, if you lose the accrued taxes which I'm temporarily forgoing, along with the rest of your reinvested earnings, I'll take the loss myself.

However, as a solution to the problem of applying the income tax to undistributed earnings, the above proposal has grave limitations. The remedy is contingent upon the acceptance of much more rigorous treatment of capital gains, which might prove about as unpopular as an undistributed-profits tax. Since this is a political objection, it might be discounted if the program were sound on other counts. More serious are the inequities involved in the proposal. Corporate income not distributed in dividends would escape the tax system entirely until, as a result of sale, gift, or death transfer, it was realized

[1] Simons, *op. cit.*

by the taxpayer in the form of a capital gain. In many cases this would involve a delay in the taxation of important additions to economic power until the taxpayer's death.[1] The timing of taxation is exceedingly important, and it is doubtful if any burdens imposed upon the dead can make up for immunities allowed the living. The difference between tax forgiveness and this long postponement of tax liability is like that between title to property and a 99-year lease. Furthermore, unless the privilege to be taxed only upon withdrawals were extended to unincorporated business (including farmers), a discrimination would be added to those already in the tax system; and if the privilege were made universal, a long step would be taken toward an income tax applied only to income used for consumption. As previously stated, it is difficult to justify preferred treatment for one kind of saving or investment as compared with another. It is probably impossible to provide identical treatment for accrued and realized economic power, but the distinction is one that should be minimized and not magnified.

The proposal to confine taxation of withheld income to the levy on realized capital gains also involves uncertain and possibly serious adverse effects upon income-tax revenues. To be sure, some gain for total revenues could be expected if all capital gains were taxed eventually at the full schedule of rates. But the capital-gains element in the income-tax base has been notoriously unstable, and the realization of capital losses is subject to manipulation. Immediate shrinkage in the tax base as the result of encouraged use of business entities for saving might be considerable.

In spite of these objections, the proposal to tax reinvested earnings only as realized capital gains has merit and deserves consideration in recasting the postwar tax system. At all events, the method might well be applied to small new busi-

[1] On the other hand, the "penalty" of higher surtaxes in prospective capital gains might exercise considerable restraint on the propensity to postpone the realization of such gains.

nesses where maximum assistance in obtaining new equity capital seems especially warranted.

3. *Confining the Corporation Tax to a Withholding Levy and an Advance Payment of Taxes for Stockholders If and While Earnings Are Retained by the Corporation for Reinvestment*

  a. Explanation. A third proposal for dealing with our problem stems from British experience. The main British tax on corporate income may be described as a combination of a withholding tax and an advance payment of taxes for stockholders if and while earnings are retained in the corporation for reinvestment. The tax carries the standard, or normal, rate that is applied to low-bracket personal income, which is one level above the substandard rate for the lowest bracket of income. The standard rate in Great Britain has been much higher than the normal rate in the United States, but our own low-bracket rate is likely to emerge from the war at a much higher level than prevailed in the past. The British tax system extends a credit to individuals for taxes paid by the corporation upon any earnings distributed. This makes the corporation tax a withholding levy. But the British tax is also paid by corporations on that portion of income which is not distributed. This is an advance payment for stockholders and is credited to them, applying on their personal tax liability if and when dividends are subsequently paid. However, it does not equate perfectly the burden upon distributed and that upon undistributed income. Were the retained income distributed to affluent stockholders, it would be subject to high surtaxes; were it distributed to individuals with large personal exemptions and small incomes, it would be subject to an effective rate lower than that applied to the corporation.

  More specifically, this proposed combination of withholding tax and advance payment upon retained income would operate as follows: Assume that the low-bracket personal tax rate is 20 per cent. Corporation *A* earns $1,000,000 in a given year, on which it pays a 20 per cent tax of $200,000. Half the remaining $800,000 is distributed, and on this the corporation levy is treated in all respects like a withholding tax; no further tax is due unless stockholders are in the higher income brackets and have surtaxes to pay. In the case of stockholders with low incomes and dependents, refunds may be due. For purposes of calculating the base of the personal tax, the withheld tax on dividends is added to the dividends received. On the $400,000 retained by the corporation, the credit for the tax paid will not be taken up until the distribution of dividends occurs or capital gains are realized by sale, gift, or death transfer of securities.

Instead of applying the lowest bracket of tax, an intermediary rate such as Great Britain maintains might be used. One recent observer advocated the application of the highest rate of personal surtax, but this seems unnecessarily drastic. Moreover, when the corporation rate becomes higher than that applicable to the lower brackets of income, the advance payment on undistributed profits acts as pressure upon management to distribute rather than retain and reinvest earnings.[1]

b. Modifications. The proposal is flexible enough to permit several additional features. No advance payment for stockholders would be required if, by a variety of possible methods, the latter assume immediately their full personal tax responsibility upon their share of the undistributed earnings. This could be accomplished by the declaration of taxable stock dividends or the issuance of other taxable securities. Or it might take the form of voluntary consent by the stockholders to taxation upon their prorata shares of corporate reinvestment.[2] In either event, the tax obligation upon the business income involved would be fully satisfied.[3]

---

[1] The proposal is compatible with but does not require a tax on intercorporate dividends. The purpose of a tax on this income is mainly to discourage holding companies. As previously observed, it is not a discriminating police measure; if attainable, other ways of controlling overcomplicated corporate structure are preferable.

[2] "Consent dividends" (see *Internal Revenue Code*, Sec. 28).

[3] Except for the capital-gains tax, which will be discussed later.

As a second special feature, new manufacturing enterprises of small size might be allowed to reinvest all (or a specified proportion) of their earnings without any advance payment. This would involve admittedly difficult problems of classification and administration, but it is recommended for consideration and trial in the hope and expectation that these difficulties might be overcome. The development, if successful, would foster new investment and new competition. It would recognize and help to counteract the present competitive disadvantage that handicaps small business in its effort to raise equity capital. Companies of small size and at an early stage of their growth find the organized capital market prohibitively expensive and funds from banks often inaccessible. That the growth of new and small enterprises is vitally important to a healthy economy is a proposition so generally recognized that no argument seems necessary to support it. Provided that it does not subsidize smallness or penalize size as such, the tax system should be used insofar as feasible to ease the special difficulties of small business.

Two problems that will be encountered in extending this special allowance to new small business should be mentioned. The first is that of defining new and small enterprise. Some experimentation would undoubtedly be helpful here. To begin with, the classification might be limited to the first 8 years of operation for new corporations not exceeding a million dollars in assets. It might be further limited to companies half of whose capital had been raised by the issue of new stock (refunding excluded) or by corporate reinvestment. The privilege should be confined to independent corporations owned exclusively, or at least predominantly, by noncorporate stockholders. The million-dollar limit is about the point at which capital can be obtained at reasonable cost in the organized capital market, and the 8-year period should give the company ample time to acquire momentum.

The second and more important difficulty concerns the discrimination that results from confining the program to *corporate* reinvestment. To extend the concession to unincorporated companies would seriously impair the universality of the personal income tax and would add greatly to the problems of definition and administration. However, the field of manufacturing is now very largely incorporated; and if the concession were confined to this area, the problem would be fairly limited in scope. Moreover, the discrimination involved in the proposal would be offset in part by the advantages of exemptions and graduated rates in the personal income tax. In any event, the concession to small new enterprises would be temporary in character and would eventually be paid for when dividends were declared or the stockholder realized capital gains on the reinvestment (at death or through gift, if not by sale).

A possible alternative modification would allow all small business, or even all business, the standing privilege of retaining a percentage of earnings without withholding tax. The allowance would act as a stimulant to business investment, and it would stand as recognition of the fact that some reinvestment is necessary merely to keep abreast of the times (in other words, to avoid "concealed obsolescence"). On the other hand, the proposal has some flavor of special privilege, and it would complicate the calculation of capital gains attributable to reinvestment (see page 81). The proposal is not recommended here, but it is submitted as one that has substantial merit. It could be held in reserve until it is apparent that stimulation of this sort is necessary.

The first of the modifications discussed in this section is definitely recommended, and the second is offered tentatively for consideration and trial.

c. Advantages and Disadvantages of the Proposal. The proposed integration of the personal and corporate taxes [described in Sec. (*a*)] is not perfect as a solution of the problems of treating undistributed profits, but it is a sensible compromise among the interests at stake. Business will not like the idea of any revival of a levy on undistributed profits; but this proposal does not constitute the undistributed-profits tax of 1936, and it would be set into a vastly changed tax system. It involves no duplication and no pressure to distribute rather than to reinvest income. It involves no drain on available capital beyond that already experienced; undistributed profits would be subject to no greater burdens than at present. The levy upon undistributed profits is simply a temporary payment on the account of individuals. As compared with the present arrangement, the proposal would eliminate the duplication of taxes; it would do away with the discrimination against stock as contrasted with credit financing; and it would aid in removing serious impediments to production and employment.

From the standpoint of the revenue, the proposal has the important advantage that it would utilize the corporation as a central source of accounting, collection, and fiscal support. Current collection on corporate reinvestment would help to reduce the revenue replacement problem involved in the elimination of the corporate tax. The proposal is in accord with the current practice of withholding and has successful precedents. It does not differ greatly from the pattern of income taxation originally established in the American law.

Among the disadvantages of the proposal is the fact that it is by no means free from administrative difficulties, particularly in allowing proper credit for withheld taxes in the case of delayed dividends and capital gains. For delayed dividends, some rule would be required to determine the sequence of earnings distributed. It might even prove desirable in the interest of simplicity to provide that, in case of rate changes, the taxpayer should be credited with the current withholding rate prevailing at the time of distribution. A capital gain attributable to reinvested earnings is much like a delayed dividend, but to credit withheld taxes on such income involves considerable complication. Perhaps the simplest procedure would be to require each company to compute and report annually the tax on undistributed profits per share of stock outstanding. The sum of such taxes during the period of stock ownership would be the tax credit to be taken up by the stockholder subsequently reporting a capital gain or loss. This procedure, while not simple, would not be prohibitively difficult. A further weakness of the proposal for withholding and advance payment is that it succeeds only partly in integrating corporate and personal taxes and in eliminating the tax advantage of corporate reinvestment where high-income stockholders are involved. It is likely, however, that this is as near to perfect integration as is feasible. Moreover, some favor for reinvestment may be regarded as a desirable stimulant. Finally, the fact that the proposal continues the corporation tax in form means that certain corporation tax problems, such as the treatment of net losses and of depreciation and obsolescence, remain. If the corporation tax could be eliminated entirely both as to form and substance, these many problems could be wiped out by one stroke of the brush. But, in the author's opinion, there is no available means to this end that would not create more problems than it would solve.

From the fiscal standpoint, integration of the corporate and personal income taxes along the lines suggested appears to offer no prohibitive difficulties. The yield of the corporate tax has usually been greater than that of the personal income tax, and obviously the loss of a major part of this revenue source would leave a sizable hole in the receipts of the federal government. It cannot be overlooked, either, that the personal income tax has some serious weaknesses on the administrative side and that moderation in this tax at all levels is desirable. However, the proposal here made has the fiscal advantage of providing for the collection of advance payments on earnings retained in the business and of discouraging the use of the corporation as a means of avoidance. Some compensation for the loss of the corporate tax would also appear in the increased dividends subject to the personal income tax. The proposal would probably mean a loss of about half the revenue now derived from corporations, and the total tax burden on the profit element in income might be reduced about one-third. Since the net income earned by corporations occupies a minor place in the whole national income (from 1921 to 1940 the ratio to national income of corporate profits before taxes, after deducting corporate losses, was 6.3 per cent), the revenue replacement problem involved in the proposal seems of manageable proportions.

F. Maintenance of a Moderate Business Tax as Such

The proposal just considered is quite compatible with the levy of a moderate corporate business tax as such.[1] The retention of any business tax is objectionable on many counts previously cited but it also has some advantages, including the following:

1. A moderate business tax could compensate in some degree for the advantage allowed corporations (as compared with partnerships, for example) in the application of less than full surtax rates to business saving.

2. A moderate business tax would contribute to the revenue substantially and involve comparatively small additional administrative expense.

3. It is likely that integration of federal corporate and personal taxes would increase considerably the profit margin to which business became accustomed during the late thirties. Some addition to this margin seems acceptable as a stimulant to business activity and as a feature of an improved tax system. However, prices and incomes in an economic system become adjusted even to bad economic arrangements. Once the adjustment has been made, precipitous changes of wide dimensions are undesirable and unlikely to accomplish their objective.[2] Movement in the direction of integration should be undertaken in several steps. Some persons will undoubtedly consider the concession recommended excessive, and maintenance of a moderate independent business tax is not a

[1] The British have had such a levy in recent years at a rate of 5 per cent.
[2] This is particularly true of public utilities, where taxes have become embedded in rate structures that cannot be changed without a substantial lag.

wholly undesirable compromise. However, an independent nonintegrated business income tax is an invitation to develop this illogical and discriminatory source to its present, or at least its prewar, place in the revenue system.[1] This would need watching.

It is recommended that the independent business tax should be eliminated entirely in several steps over a period of years. Gradual reduction of the business tax would facilitate the timing of tax changes to meet postwar pressures of inflation; it would probably constitute a more sustained and more powerful stimulus to business than would an immediate elimination. A moderate independent levy might be retained until fiscal conditions permitted further change. The main corporate tax should be integrated with the personal tax as rapidly as possible.

G. Conclusion

A combination of the three alternative solutions for treating undistributed profits is thus recommended. The partnership method would be applied to personal holding companies and corporations "improperly" accumulating surplus. Other companies might be permitted to use this system on an optional basis. The capital-gains method would be applied to new enterprises of small size. The withholding-advance-payment system would be applied to most corporations.

The objective of integrating the corporate and personal taxes should not be lost, however, in the debate on specific methods. This modification is the most urgent of all changes needed for the adaptation of the tax structure to our postwar production and employment requirements.

[1] See the history of the federal corporation income tax, page 18.

IV. EXCESS-PROFITS TAX REPEAL

THE excess-profits tax should be repealed soon after the end of the war, the repeal to take effect a year later. The declared-value capital-stock excess-profits-tax combination should be repealed now.

The present excess-profits tax is set up as an emergency measure and is worded in such a manner as to indicate the absence of any intent to carry it beyond the war. However, there will undoubtedly be a demand for a retention of the tax in the peacetime taxation system much like the demand following the last war. Moreover, the timing of the repeal, if repeal is to be the outcome, involves some difficult questions of postwar fiscal policy. For these and other reasons, the future treatment of the excess-profits tax warrants an important place in any postwar taxation program.

1. EXCESS-PROFITS TAX DURING THE WAR

An excess-profits tax during this war was a political necessity. Governmental control of the private economy has largely taken the form of freezing or attempting to freeze prewar economic relations, including the prices of finished products, raw materials, and labor. The profits tax, with its 95 per cent rate and its emphasis upon the prewar experience of each company, aimed at a near freeze in the area of profits not very different from that applied elsewhere in the economy. Such a tax was required to satisfy the demands of those who were involved at other points in the freezing process. It was an answer to the natural demand for some counterpart to the sacrifices being made by persons in the armed forces. Moreover, it was a response to the feeling that the state should share in the profits (at least the extraordinary profits) created by its own extraordinary outlay. Competitive checks upon excessive earnings, which are normally operative (even though not too perfectly) in times of peace, are largely suspended during a war because of the extreme urgency of much of the demand. Many of the risks of production normally assumed by private business are shifted to the government.

2. EXCESS-PROFITS TAX IN PEACETIME

The strongest ground for including the excess-profits tax in the peacetime tax system is that the tax affords an opportunity to recapture part of the excessive gains resulting from monopolistic business.

The monopoly problem will undoubtedly need increased attention in the postwar world, for it is a matter of common knowledge that the war has encouraged industrial concentration. Competition is a fairly adequate policing force in the economic system when most production is carried on by numerous small units, but it is not dependable when a few large companies dominate many fields. These few concerns tend to set prices by joint action; or, with similar results, they act with conscious regard for the effect of their own price policies upon their "competitors." It is true that competition is still a very lively corpse; there are many businessmen who believe it was never so vigorous and effective. In addition to some competition within the same line, there is very active interproduct rivalry. Thus, plastics threaten wood and steel as construction materials; electricity supplants gas; mail-order houses invade the department-store field with competitive services; and so on. Exactly what this adds up to is not clear, but it obviously is something less than adequate protection for the consumer.

Unfortunately for the application of the excess-profits tax as a solution to this problem, there is no clear way to isolate monopoly profits. If there were, such gains could probably be prevented from occurring in the first place. We know that, in an ideal order free from monopoly, profits would differ among concerns because of varying degrees of risk inherent in different lines of business, because of unforeseen developments (or noneconomic factors, such as war) causing maladjustments between demand and supply, and because of differences in the efficiency of management. We know, also, that in the real world there are further variations in profits caused by limitations on competition resulting from monopolistic practices and also from such pervasive conditions as differentiation of product, ignorance of buyers and sellers, and the costs of communication and transportation. No doubt there are unnecessary rewards in this picture, but no satisfactory technique for singling them out has yet been devised.

There are many ways, other than by taxation of profits, to attack the monopoly problem. Fewer barriers to foreign trade (lower tariffs) is one of the surest and soundest. In addition, an active and discriminating federal judicial and administrative supervision of trade practices and business combinations is needed. A federal incorporation franchise for interstate companies has been long overdue. Perhaps the development of an effective cooperative movement is the answer. Perhaps the tax system can be used to foster competition by supporting small or new business. Both intelligence and courage are needed to master this problem, and none of the approaches to a solution should be lightly dismissed. But the excess-profits tax seems much too crude an instrument to be employed effectively in this role.

More important than the recapture of monopoly gains in the postwar world will be the prevention of monopoly restriction of output. But this is a job for the legislative police power and not for the tax system.

As previously observed, an excess-profits tax applies to the marginal segments of income (those above the credits). For this reason, among others, it discourages the incentives for risk-taking and expansion on the one hand and for efficiency and conservation on the other. No techniques in excess-profits taxation have been devised to allow for differences in the risk factor or for superior efficiency of management. It is worth noting that, if an American business now launches an advertising campaign, 80 per cent of the cost of such an outlay may be financed in effect by the federal government.[1] Many other outlays can be similarly financed. Thriftiness and spendthriftiness are both shorn of meaning when a tax reduces the gain or loss to 20 cents on the dollar. While patriotism might be relied upon to sustain the imposition of heavy taxes on profits during the war, a similar reliance in times of peace might be hazardous.

The tax may also penalize companies with irregular income. The fortunate concern that earns 8 per cent regularly may have no tax to pay, while the one that alternates between a 16 per cent return and no income may be taxed substantially. It is because of such effects, particularly adverse to growing small companies, that the tax is said by its critics to foster rather than discourage monopoly. It may be possible to make due allowance for risk and efficiency in an excess-profits tax, but the problem has thus far defied solution.

One of the weakest spots in the armor of an excess-profits tax lies in the technical difficulties in its application. No one can be very enthusiastic about a tax measure that distributes the rewards of the economic process mainly according to luck or political (as contrasted with economic) efficiency. This is the danger that lurks in the excess-profits tax, although undoubtedly the techniques of applying this tax have improved since we last experimented with it twenty-five years ago. The arbitrariness and the anomalies are, however, still conspicuous. To choose a few at random: Why should the concern operating on borrowed capital have the privilege of including half of such capital in the tax base (for calculating the return on invested capital), whereas a firm that rents its capital has no such privilege?[2] Why should a personal service corporation

[1] It is true that the Treasury exercises some check on advertising outlays, but this does not invalidate the illustration.

[2] The discrimination existing in some cases is alleviated but not eliminated by the fact that only half of interest paid is deductible in calculating excess profits.

escape the excess-profits tax on the ground that its income is mostly from services rather than capital, when many other taxable corporations show the same characteristic but only to a lesser degree? Why should a developing corporation be taxed on the theory that its increased profits are due to the war, while a declining corporation, which may have received a lift because of the war, escapes? Most important of all, of course, are the great and thus far insurmountable difficulties in differentiating for risk. Relief provision, the carry-over and carry-back of unused excess-profits credit, and other refinements have helped to make the present law less arbitrary than that in force during the last war; but the staunchest friend of the tax would not contend that the technical problems of application are anywhere near solution.

Anyone who studies the multitudinous points of subtle distinction and classification involved in an excess-profits tax cannot fail to be impressed with the great possibilities for injustice and unfair competitive advantage inherent in its application. An exceedingly complicated law is necessary to cover the varied conditions to which it must apply, and much has to be left, even then, to administrative discretion. These complexities are illustrated by the provisions dealing with business reorganization, which are so involved that they are utterly incomprehensible to the layman. High compliance costs and much litigation attend such legislation. The historical approach to the definition of capital (one of the bases of calculating exemptions from the excess-profits tax) is probably the best that could be devised, but it involves resurrecting and recasting in part a multitude of records that were regarded as buried. In 1940, when the profits tax was under consideration, there were cases still pending in the courts dealing with the determination of capital under the 1918 law. Annual accounting is inherently tentative, provisional, and inexact, and it is hard put to give the precise answers required by a 95 per cent excess-profits tax.

In summary and conclusion, the excess-profits tax, at least in its present state of imperfection, had best be reserved for war application. Its peacetime employment might be very inimical to risky enterprise and to business efficiency. Its impact upon marginal income would make it a temptation to waste resources. As an antidote for monopoly, it would not be sufficiently discriminating to achieve its purpose, and it could do much damage in the attempt. For the present, we are obliged to attack the monopoly problem with other weapons, however inadequate they may be.

3. TIMING THE REPEAL OF THE TAX

If the excess-profits tax is to be ruled out of the peacetime tax system, the question still remains as to when the tax should be dropped. There will be strong demand for such action as soon as hostilities have ceased. This will be supported by the valid contention that a profits tax unsustained by war patriotism will lead to waste and will weaken the incentives to convert business facilities to an efficient peacetime basis. On the other hand, the problem of inflation may enter an acute phase immediately after the war, when buying power will have a long start over the production of civilian goods. While the excess-profits tax is not in itself a very effective deflationary measure, involving as it does some inflationary tendencies, it is a politically significant part of a general control program. Immediate elimination of the excess-profits tax would be the signal for a relaxation of wage and price controls. Normal competitive conditions will not be restored overnight after the war. The agricultural market will reflect a strong war influence until the important task of food relief for the war-devastated countries is accomplished. Business itself will not assume normal operation for a considerable period—materials from abroad will not become available immediately, and varying periods required for conversion will create different effects upon profits.

Under these circumstances the sensible procedure would be to repeal the excess-profits tax at the close of hostilities with provision for the repeal to take effect later. This would give much the same lift to business as an immediate repeal without prematurely letting down the bars of war controls. After the repeal is made effective, the administration of the law should be continued to permit the carry-back of losses and excess-profits credits until the main effects of war conversion and reconversion have been liquidated. The present law contains no commitment that this will be done, but it is in keeping with the accepted view that true war profits should be determined for the whole war period, including the period in which the effects of the war are being liquidated.

4. DECLARED-VALUE EXCESS-PROFITS TAX

Mention should be made of another, but not very important, institution in the excess-profits tax field, namely, the combined declared-value, capital-stock, and excess-profits taxes surviving from prewar origin in the Industrial Recovery Act of 1933. Through the connection of excess profits to net income and of declared-value capital stock to excess profits, these taxes, in ways that need not here be explained, amount to an additional levy on net income. They add little to the tax system but complication, extra compliance costs, and occasionally capricious results, and they are especially inimical to small companies. Calculation for these taxes is carried on in an artificial atmosphere all but divorced from reality; they are a lawyer's plaything rather than a producer's levy; and they serve principally as a monument to the misdirected ingenuity of tax-makers. They represent the sort of complication in the tax system that ought to be avoided in the future, and they should be repealed certainly not later than the end of the war. More could be said for a genuine capital-stock tax, but it involves some of the same administrative vagaries as the excess-profits tax.

5. CONCLUSION

In conclusion, it can be asserted that an undistributed-profits tax is a far more promising candidate for a place in the permanent tax system than an excess-profits tax. Because of the unfortunate experience of 1936, the undistributed-profits tax is in disfavor with many businessmen, but the character of that experience was due to a badly conceived law rather than to an unsound fundamental objective. A sensible answer to the business tax problem is more likely to be found along the road we then opened, although with inauspicious results, than on the road of excess-profits taxation we have been forced to travel during the war years. Best of all, as we have indicated, would be the opening of a new road to the integration of corporate and personal taxes.

V. MORE GENEROUS ALLOWANCE
FOR BUSINESS LOSSES

A CARRY-OVER of at least 6 years for net business losses should be allowed.[1] This provision for losses should apply to unincorporated as well as incorporated business.

The characteristics of business losses must be recognized in formulating federal tax policy. Among these characteristics the following are especially relevant:

1. Fear of possible loss is often more important in business decisions involving large uncertainties than the hope of positive profit. Businessmen are willing to continue operation of their enterprises at times when prospect of profit is small, providing they do not by so doing incur too great a risk of loss.[2] During the last war a prominent critic[3] went so far as to suggest postwar government absorption of business losses in order to encourage the continuation of production at wartime levels.

2. A business income tax that is paid on current income before the accumulated deficits of previous years have been absorbed is really paid out of capital rather than out of income.

3. New and small businesses are less profitable as a group than large and established concerns, and the range of profitability and loss is much wider.[4]

4. The equipment industries, which are especially sensitive to business cycles and shifts in business confidence, are particularly susceptible to losses in depression years.

[1] A subsequent recommendation calls for the averaging of personal income over a period of years. This would extend to wage earners who may suffer from unemployment an equivalent to the carry-over and carry-back of business losses.

[2] David Friday, "Maintaining Productive Output," *Journal of Political Economy*, Vol. XXVII, January, 1919, pp. 117–126.

[3] *Ibid.*

[4] William Leonard Crum, *Corporate Size and Earning Power*, Harvard University Press, 1939.

5. The degree and scope of corporate losses, both in good and in bad years, are rarely fully appreciated. Had all American corporations been allowed to file a joint consolidated return with an unlimited carry-over and carry-back of losses from 1922 to 1939, their net income as reported would have been reduced 45.7 per cent.[1]

6. Incompetence of management is sometimes responsible for losses, but market fluctuations and other impersonal factors are of at least equal importance.

Of course, a net income tax allows the business losses in a given year and for a given company to be offset against the corresponding business gains—it would not otherwise be a *net income tax*. The problem concerns the treatment of *net business losses*. A carry-over of such losses (for limited periods, never longer than 2 years), so that they may be offset against the net business gains of subsequent years, has been provided intermittently by the federal tax system. A carry-over provision was introduced in 1919 and remained in the federal revenue act until the Industrial Recovery Act of 1933. During the period of heavy losses in the thirties, businesses were without the benefit of this provision. It was reintroduced in 1939; and, in 1942, a carry-back of 2 years was added. The carry-back was based on the theory that certain postwar losses from reconversion should be taken into account in appraising the true net gains made by business during the war years. It means that the tax calculations of the best years of the war may be reopened and scaled downward to take account of the effects of early postwar changes. This represents a substantial concession to business and one that is thoroughly sound.

The British have been much more generous in their tax treatment of business losses than has the United States. The Royal Commission on Income Tax (1920) recommended a 6-year carry-over, and this recommendation was adopted in 1926. Prior to 1926 a 3-year moving average of income had

[1] Calculation based on *Statistics of Income*, United States Treasury Department.

been in effect, and the British had experimented with even longer periods for reckoning business income. The shift from the averaging system to a carry-over for losses was recommended by the Royal Commission, which observed that "Hardly anyone has a good word for the average." The Act of 1932 extended the carry-over of losses beyond 6 years by permitting the deduction, without limits as to time, of either the balance of the loss, or the total depreciation set off within the 6 years in priority to such loss, whichever is less. The British are reputed to have a "tough" tax system, but in many respects it is sounder than our own.

From the standpoint of income-tax theory and support for business motivation, an indefinite carry-over of losses would be ideal. However, this would probably be unworkable administratively and would involve problems in cases of mergers and reorganizations. Some "statute of limitations" is probably required, but it should cover a carry-over period of not less than 6 years. According to one study of the subject,[1] even a 6-year period would have been insufficient during the thirties to allow full credit for losses to as many as one-third of equipment manufacturing companies. No distinction need be made between individual and corporate business with regard to the carry-over.

Companies with large nondeductible net losses pay a higher effective rate of income tax than companies with more regular income. This places a special burden upon risk-taking, which is precisely what an intelligent government, interested in a dynamic economy and a high employment level, should avoid. During the thirties, the effective rate of the federal income tax on companies producing capital goods was found by one study[2] to range from the statutory rate schedule to over 100 per cent. The effective rate on companies producing consumption goods was generally much less. There is no princi-

[1] Machinery and Allied Products Institute, *Capital Goods Industries and Federal Income Tax*, 1940.
[2] *Ibid.*

ple of taxation, either in terms of equity or in terms of effects on production, that warrants such a discrimination. Here again the major canons of taxation point in the same direction. Considerations of immediate adequacy of revenue may seem to argue against this change, but governments as well as individuals need to give some heed to their long-run interests. It will be strong evidence that this lesson has been learned if in the postwar period the government keeps faith with its present program of carry-over and carry-back for war and reconversion losses. Based on the experience of 1933, skepticism as to the likelihood of this occurring is already widely felt by businessmen. It would bolster business morale if this skepticism were laid to rest.

Much could be said for a carry-back as well as a carry-over of losses. If both were allowed without limitation, the income tax would be confined to the real earnings of a company during its life operation. In order to avoid refunds and other complications,[1] however, and because the taxation of profits without the possibility of offset against future losses is usually regarded as less prejudicial than taxation without allowance for prior losses, the carry-back is not recommended as a permanent part of our tax system.

[1] Particularly in the calculation of advance payments to be credited at the time a capital gain is realized. See page 81.

VI. MORE FREEDOM IN DEPRECIATION AND OBSOLESCENCE ACCOUNTING

MORE latitude in the timing of deductions for depreciation and obsolescence should be granted. Less attention to the calendar year in income-tax accounting would reduce the argument and litigation over the proper amounts of depreciation and obsolescence attributable to the operation of any one period. Shortening the write-off period for these impairments of capital value promotes economic progress by reducing resistance to the installation of improved equipment. Accelerated depreciation (as in the present 5-year amortization provision for certain war capital) could be used to promote investment during a depression, and, in extreme cases, its use for such purposes is recommended.

1. NATURE OF AND ALLOWANCE FOR IMPAIRMENT OF CAPITAL

The income-tax laws accept the proposition that receipts may not be considered income until an allowance has been made for impairment of capital. Impairment may occur in a number of ways: (1) By depreciation; assets may wear out as a result of service. (2) By obsolescence; capital may become antiquated or out-of-date. (3) By depletion; capital may be sold, piece by piece, as in the case of mineral and forest resources. Maintenance and repairs are expenses incurred in avoiding impairment of capital and are sometimes and to some extent an offset against depreciation.

Stated very generally, the federal income-tax statute provides for deduction from gross income of "a reasonable allowance for the exhaustion, wear and tear of property used in the trade or business." The regulations add that the proper allowance is one which, if calculated on a reasonable plan, will, when added to the salvage value, equal the cost or "total basis" of the property. In principle, the rate of deduction is not required to be uniform. "Normal obsolescence" is treated as a part of depreciation. This includes impairment of capital resulting from predictable improvements or changes introduced from time to time in the art or industry generally. Another form of obsolescence is the sudden loss of useful value due to a particular invention or a change in demand. The second type is regarded as unpredictable until the loss is "realized."

2. ESTIMATES OF DEPRECIATION NECESSARILY INEXACT

It is generally agreed that depreciation is, at best, a matter of rough estimate. The calculation involves so many variables and imponderables that it may be closer to guesswork than estimating. Competent judges will often disagree substantially as to what the allowance should be. The equipment may have one useful life as an active element in production and another if its term of usefulness as "stand-by" equipment is taken into account. The value sought to be recovered may be the original investment, modified or unmodified for a price trend, or the cost of an asset that will maintain output or profit-making capacity. Allowances must be made for maintenance and normal obsolescence, the latter depending on the prospective rate of invention and, to some extent, on the wages and efficiency of labor. Once the time and value dimensions of depreciation are determined, there remains finally the decision as to how it shall be spread over the years. For this there are available several alternative procedures.

In 1934, a congressional committee reported that depreciation allowances were amounting to several times the net income of corporations and that the 1930 allowances were about half again as large as those of 1924. From this slender evidence, it was concluded that corporations were "padding" their depreciation returns, and legislation to reduce allowances by 25 per cent was proposed. The legislation was dropped on assurance from the Treasury that allowances would be reduced by administrative action. This involved a small immediate gain[1] for the Treasury, but it was not the sort of program to accelerate industrial recovery during a depression.

3. MORE FREEDOM RECOMMENDED

The carry-over of losses, with its resulting diminished emphasis upon annual accounting, would make possible greater freedom in determining deductions for depreciation and obsolescence. Much litigation and argument would be happily avoided or reduced by less attention to the timing of these deductions. Unfortunately, the trend is in the opposite direction. Expense for research, which formerly was deductible on a cash basis when incurred, is required by a recent ruling to be capitalized and spread over the years of usefulness of the results of the research. This may be fiscally productive in the short run, but it is not the way to encourage industrial progress. In fact, because the trend of corporate tax rates has continued upward, the government probably has lost revenue by administrative reductions in current depreciation charges. The government's principal concern should be to ascertain that the cost of fixed facilities is deducted in an orderly manner and that safeguards are established to prevent duplicate deductions. It certainly seems in order to suggest that, within a wide range of tolerance, business's own judgment with reference to depreciation and obsolescence, as indicated by its books, might well be accepted in lieu of a more precise figure laboriously calculated by the Bureau of Internal Revenue.

[1] All assets must eventually be depreciated in full in any case. This differs from the case of depletion, where allowances have not only been extremely generous but are so computed that they may eventually add up to more than the full cost of the assets.

4. ACCELERATED DEPRECIATION

Corporations replace old equipment and expand total equipment at irregular and varying rates. Space does not permit a discussion of why managements make affirmative decisions on these matters when they do. It can be said, however, that decisions as to replacements are more likely to be affirmative when assets are considerably depreciated on a company's books. Decisions favorable to expansion are also encouraged by rapid depreciation because uncertainties are reduced if a large part of the cost of new equipment can be written off and the capital cost recovered in the early years of its use.

During the war, industry was given the privilege of amortizing certain new equipment over a 5-year period. Although the government still found it necessary to supply a large part of the capital for war expansion, the amortization program was effective in removing impediments to the installation of new equipment. This technique of encouraging expansion can be used in peacetime as well as in wartime. The government, in most cases, would suffer a postponement rather than a loss of taxes. The postponement of taxes on income currently earned would, however, be at some risk to the government and might create some strain upon its current budget. This type of program might be used effectively as a depression remedy, and it should be held in reserve for such application in extreme cases.

VII. ROLE OF AND CHANGES IN THE PERSONAL INCOME TAX

IF BUSINESS taxation is to be deemphasized after the war, some other element in the tax system must be given a more important role. The principal candidates for this are personal taxation (personal income and death taxes) and indirect consumption, or sales, taxes. Of these the author prefers personal taxation as the major source of revenue in the post-war federal tax system. The arguments supporting this choice will be elaborated later. It may be observed here, however, that the personal income tax is a logical substitute for the corporate income tax, since abandonment or deemphasis of the corporate tax is recommended on the ground that it should be integrated with the personal tax. Regressive taxes at the state and local levels are probably inevitable; but the federal government, with its more adequate fiscal powers, should avoid these taxes in the main, confining them, as a rule, to the special excises on nonessential consumption.

1. BROAD BASE

Both for adequacy of revenue and for the sake of discipline, a broad base should be retained in the income tax after the war. A direct personal tax with wide participation provides a wholesome way for a democracy to finance its many public services, and it helps disillusion those who like to think the government is an exception to the rule that "you can't get something for nothing." Collection of a direct federal tax from no more than four million taxpayers (in 1939) was a flagrant political abuse of what should be the most equitable means of raising revenue. Along with direct taxation of large numbers of people, collection at the source, current payment, and other devices to facilitate payment and collection should be retained and improved. Reductions in the standard rates of tax, if any, should be conservative; relief for the low-income groups should take the form of lightening special excises and repeal of the federal sales tax, if this becomes part of the federal tax system during the war. A shift from business to personal taxes, by bringing tax burdens into the open and by extending the scope of the personal tax with its exemptions and progressive rates, will also benefit the recipients of lower incomes.

The low-bracket income-tax rates and exemptions now employed are at levels that would have been appropriate for prewar use. Accordingly, they are inadequate for the present emergency. One advantage of raising these taxes to levels consonant with immediate revenue needs is that it facilitates the continuance of adequate personal taxation after the war.

2. IMPROVED ADMINISTRATION

If the personal income tax is to play the major role in postwar financing, more investment must be made in the improvement of its administration. No doubt a high percentage of persons will report honestly and pay without compulsion what they consider to be a fair tax. Unhappily, however, experience has shown that respect for the obligations of citizenship is not a sufficient basis for the administration of any tax. This is particularly true when taxes are at the high levels that postwar exigencies will require. A large proportion of income is subject to adequate check through information furnished at the source and through auditing, but the considerable income of professional persons, independent businessmen, and farmers cannot be satisfactorily verified in this manner. Much of the income of such persons is known only to the recipient, his secretary, and God. Two of these parties are sometimes corruptible, and the third has never been particularly concerned with income-tax administration. There are devices by which these incomes can be checked with tolerable adequacy. Some of these devices are more highly developed in the best state income-tax administrations than in that of the federal government. Federal administration has operated on the misguided principle that income-tax policing should be largely confined to spots where it yields large returns for the outlay. But adequate income-tax policing is essential for the broader objectives of fairness and the maintenance of taxpayers' morale. Even in the interest of total revenue we should spend much more on direct enforcement. Enforcement activities serve to increase payments from taxpayers other than those brought to book. The problem has been precipitated during the war by the revolutionary expansion in scope of the income tax, and meeting it squarely cannot for long be avoided by relying on war patriotism to ensure honest tax returns. In the postwar period, it will be necessary either to provide adequate administration of the personal income tax or to rely on much less equitable and otherwise less desirable forms of taxation. The income tax without adequate administration will degenerate into an unfair tax largely on wages and dividends.

Accountants and businessmen are almost unanimous in the view that the government has shown more interest in squeezing an extra dollar from the taxpayer than in giving him a square deal. It is often alleged that auditors are promoted on the basis of their tax recoveries and that businessmen deliberately falsify their accounts in order to "have something for the auditor to find." Where there is so much smoke, there must be some fire; and even if these views were invalid, the fact that they exist indicates very bad government-taxpayer relations. A vigorous and intelligent program to improve these relations should be a first order of business in tax administration.[1]

---

[1] Arnold Barr has suggested to the author that the income tax and, in fact, the whole tax system might be removed from politics to some extent by delegating to a representative commission the task of preparing recommended revisions of the tax law. This could be done either regularly or at intervals. Of course, final authority on revisions would rest, as now, with Congress and the President. The suggestion merits attention.

3. REDUCTION OF SURTAXES

Some moderation is warranted in the personal tax schedule as it applies to the upper and middle levels of income, where top rates are now as high as 90 per cent.   To be compatible with the social interest in the investment of high incomes in risk-bearing securities, these rates should be reduced a quarter or a third, or the higher rates should be confined to levels of income at which relatively small amounts of potential investment capital exist.   Taking 90 per cent of the marginal dollar of high incomes tends to dissuade those who can and should invest in stocks and causes them to invest in high-grade bonds or to hoard cash.   A steeply graduated personal tax makes the margin of return between risky and safe investments so slim that there is no inducement to try the risky investment. Thus, a 20 per cent yield on stocks is reduced by a 90 per cent tax to a net yield of 2 per cent—less than the yield on many government bonds and insufficient to justify taking much risk. (See Table III)

TABLE III

EFFECT OF THE PRESENT PERSONAL TAX SYSTEM ON THE NET YIELD OF
INVESTMENTS AT THE MARGIN OF A $200,000 INCOME

Investment yield before tax, per cent	Yield after deducting 90 per cent tax	Differential yield after tax, per cent	
		Compared with yield after tax on 2 per cent bond	Compared with yield on a tax-exempt 2 per cent bond
2	0.2	0.0	−1.8
8	0.8	0.6	−1.2
12	1.2	1.0	−0.8
16	1.6	1.4	−0.4
20	2.0	1.8	0.0
30	3.0	2.8	1.0

Moderation is a virtue to be urged in government, among other reasons because it avoids the dangers of swinging from one extreme to another. (A constitutional amendment suggested by some state legislatures to limit income and death taxes to 25 per cent is a sample of such extremes.) Loopholes in the collection of income taxes are known to exist. More would be accomplished by plugging these than by setting surtax rates so high that they defeat themselves.

On the other hand, some restraint in reducing surtaxes will be required if the maintenance of an adequate standard rate is to win support. Substantial progression in rates is required to give due weight to valid interest in a more nearly equal distribution of income after taxes. Despite the stimulus to investment and expansion that is sought in this and other recommended tax changes, a disproportion between consumer demand and savings—a shortage of the former and an excess of the latter—is likely to plague us for some time. Use of the tax system to modify this unbalance is desirable. Some net stimulus to enterprise could be had by combining a considerable reduction in surtax rates with a more effective death tax, since the latter is less a curb on risk-taking and business expansion than the income tax. As will be explained later, the death tax can be substantially strengthened without increasing the rates.

It may be argued that the interest in tax moderation, stressed in this report, is as important at the lowest levels of income taxation as at the highest and that revenue requirements prevent concessions at both ends of the scale. A good tax base in the form of a large national income would help to avoid excessive taxation in all brackets. But in this connection it must be remembered that (1) it is in the low and middle brackets of income that the main flow of income occurs and the greatest fiscal potential exists; (2) the limitation of direct taxation to relatively few persons before the war was an unsound and unwholesome situation, needing correction; and (3) actual average rates of taxation in the low brackets are much lower than the marginal rates because of personal exemptions. (See Table IV.)

Role of and Changes in the Personal Income Tax

TABLE IV

AMOUNT OF INDIVIDUAL INCOME TAX, EFFECTIVE AVERAGE RATE, AND MARGINAL RATE ON NET INCOME RANGING FROM THE LOWEST TO THE HIGHEST BRACKET UNDER THE PRESENT LAW*

(Married person, no dependents. Exemption: normal and surtax, $1200. Victory tax, $624)

Net income before personal exemption	Amount of tax†	Effective average tax rate†, per cent	Marginal tax rate‡ per cent
$ 1,000	$ 15	1.5	22
1,250	29	2.3	22
1,500	79	5.3	22
1,750	134	7.7	22
2,000	188	9.4	25
2,250	242	10.8	25
2,500	297	11.9	25
2,750	351	12.8	25
3,000	405	13.5	25
4,000	647	16.2	29
5,000	894	17.9	29
6,000	1,173	19.6	33
8,000	1,780	22.3	37
10,000	2,467	24.7	41
15,000	4,533	30.2	49
20,000	7,100	35.5	58
25,000	10,035	40.1	61
50,000	27,075	54.2	75
75,000	46,955	62.6	81
100,000	68,584	68.6	88
500,000	440,747	88.1	91
1,000,000	899,000	89.9	91
5,000,000	4,499,000	90.0	91

*Source: Adapted from Exhibit I, Tables 1 and 2, Treasury Department, Division of Tax Research, Oct. 4, 1943.

† The net income subject to the victory tax is assumed to be ten-ninths of the net income before the personal exemption is deducted.

‡ Includes 3 per cent victory tax, 6 per cent normal tax, and surtax applicable to bracket.

It is evident that the modifications here proposed would create a tax system more dominantly progressive[1] than that which prevailed before the war. In 1938, at least 55 per cent of federal income came from regressive sources (assuming that the corporate tax is half progressive and half regressive). Had these modifications been in effect, not more than a third of the revenue (and probably considerably less) would have come from regressive sources.

A T.N.E.C. study of the incidence of the federal tax system[2] concluded that the federal tax system for 1938–1939 was mildly regressive for incomes up to $3000 and not markedly progressive until incomes of over $5000 were reached. With the proposed broader base and the more prominent role of the personal income tax, progression would probably begin as low as the $1000 incomes and might become characteristic of the entire income scale. The obvious and certain way to make a tax system generally and consistently progressive is by raising most of the revenue with a broadly based personal income tax.

4. ELIMINATION OF TAX-EXEMPT SECURITIES

Considerations of both equity and incentive condemn the continued maintenance of the great income-tax storm cellar, tax-exempt bonds. It is not possible here to examine all the arguments involved in this issue, but the most pertinent for the problem of production and employment expansion is that tax exemption favors the most secure form of investment. Relative as well as absolute burdens are important; and, in exempting government bonds while taxing and double-taxing risk capital, a perverse influence is exerted upon the invest-

[1] The term "progressive" is used to describe a scale of relative burdens in which higher proportions of income are paid in taxes as income advances. The term "regressive" is used to describe an opposite set of relationships in which lower proportions of income are paid in taxes as income advances. Thus the income tax is progressive because the ratio of tax to income increases as income increases. The cigarette tax is regressive because the ratio of tax to income decreases as income increases.

[2] Gerhard Colm and Helen Tarasov, "Who Pays the Taxes?," *Temporary National Economic Committee, Monograph* 3, 1940, p. 6.

ment pattern. From the standpoint of incentives, any system so modifying the natural order of things that the recipient of a $200,000 income gets the same yield after taxes on a 2 per cent government bond as on a stock bringing in 20 per cent is condemned on the face of it. From the standpoint of equity, no good word can be said for tax exemption. The principle of universality, calling for the inclusion of all types of income in the tax base, should be generally respected with as few exceptions as possible.

The interests of two groups—state and local governments and present security holders—have protected this familiar means of tax escape. Because of the artificial demand created for their securities by tax exemption, state and local governments are able to obtain their loan funds at very low rates of interest. Consequently, they oppose any change. Security holders who purchased low-yielding state and local bonds on the assumption that the privileged status of these securities would continue also defend these tax immunities. Interest on federal bonds (except on those issued before 1941, on which the federal government is bound by contract until a refunding occurs) is now taxable under the federal law. Compensation for these vested interests might take the form of an allowance to state and local governments for increased interest required on new issues or an allowance to security holders in order to compensate them for the reduction in effective yield because of cancellation of the tax-exemption privilege. If such compensation is necessary to rid us of the tax-exempt bonds, the outlay would be well warranted. Ending tax exemption on new issues would be a step forward, but complete elimination of the exemption privilege is highly desirable.

5. CLASSIFIED INCOME TAX

A case could be made for a classified income tax with preferential treatment for income derived from, or invested in, stocks. This would be on the theory that "the tax system should distinguish between incomes derived from *giving* jobs and incomes derived from *holding* jobs and should tax incomes derived from giving jobs, that is, from innovation and experimentation, at substantially lower rates than income of the same size derived from salaries."[1] Supporting this view is the hypothesis, previously mentioned, that investment is more sensitive to attack by taxation than services compensated with salaries. However, stocks differ in the degree of "innovation and experimentation" that can be credited to their owners. An even stronger objection to the proposal is that the classified income tax, departing as it does from the principles of universality and neutrality in taxation, leads back to the system of penalties and subsidies, which are so easily abused and from which we are here seeking to free ourselves. One special privilege, even though warranted, is likely to lead to another quite indefensible one. A favorable classification for dividends would involve the question of whether a similar favor should be extended to the business income of unincorporated businesses and farmers. Classification of income is not readily compatible with a graduation of rates according to the quantity of income. The combination is likely to result (as it has in European countries) in a tax system distinguished principally for its complication. Moreover, the case of preferred treatment for dividends involves the element of income most given to concentration and most significant from the standpoint of economic power. On the whole, a reasonable reduction in the higher surtaxes—a move toward moderation —seems a better means of relieving the risk-taker. Elimination of the duplication in personal and corporate taxation involves relief, both sound and specific, for the equity investor.

[1] Sumner Slichter, "Social Security after the War," Winthrop Ames Memorial Lecture, Radcliffe College, Apr. 4, 1943.

VIII. CAPITAL GAINS AND LOSSES

1. RECOMMENDATIONS

THERE should be no segregation or other limitation on the deductibility of capital losses, and net losses occasioned by such deductibility should be subject to carry-over privileges. Either by averaging income over a period of years or by other feasible provisions, due allowance should be made for the fact that capital gains and losses often accrue over long periods; they should not be treated as though they arose from a single year's operations. (A longer span for reckoning income-tax liability would also reduce tax avoidance by manipulation of capital losses.) A capital gain attributable to the reinvestment of corporate income is the equivalent of a delayed or liquidating dividend, and due allowance should be made for the taxes already paid by the corporation on such income. If adequate provisions are enacted for averaging income over a period of years, if full credit is allowed for corporate taxes on undistributed profits, and if personal surtax rates are reduced to reasonable levels, then capital gains *and losses* can, and should, be treated for tax purposes like other income. Until these basic modifications, here recommended, are made in the tax laws, some form of segregation and special treatment of capital gains and losses may be desirable.

Transfers at death or by gift should be considered as a "realization" of the fair appraised value by the donor or decedent. Windfalls that might result from the sale of stocks at prices increased as a result of the integration of the corporate and personal taxes would be fully subject to tax as capital gains.

2. PAST AND PRESENT TREATMENT

The treatment of capital gains and losses (usually gains or losses incidental to the sale of securities or real estate) is one of the most difficult issues in personal income taxation. The canons of simplicity and stability have been violated frequently, and often severely, in laws covering capital gains and losses. The main methods for the taxation of capital gains include treatment of such gains like other income with no deduction for losses, taxation with full allowance for losses, and classified taxation of gains with losses deductible only against gains of a similar class. The reduction of gains and losses by percentages dependent upon the length of time the assets have been held by the taxpayer, the application of maximum rates, and various provisions for the carry-over of losses not currently usable to offset gains have provided additional refinements. These features have been used in various combinations during the past twenty years. The present tax treatment classifies gains and losses as short-term when the assets to which they pertain have been held not over 6 months. Short-term gains are taxed like other income. Long-term gains either may be reduced to 50 per cent of their amount in reckoning income subject to the regular tax, or they may be taxed separately at a maximum rate of 25 per cent. The treatment of losses is parallel except that (whether long-term or short-term) they can be deducted from capital gains in full and from other income up to a maximum of $1000. Moreover, a 5-year carry-over of unused losses is permitted. The treatment of capital gains and losses in the case of corporations is generally similar (including the provision of a maximum rate of 25 per cent on long-term gains), but there are some differences, such as the absence of the percentage reduction.

3. KINDS AND FORMS OF CAPITAL GAINS

Capital gains are a complex phenomenon. In the case of common stocks, such gains may be due, in whole or in part, to reinvested corporate income. Such reinvestment, unless capitalized by the issuance of new securities, will tend to result in an increase in the value of stocks. This increase will be realized by the stockholder at the time of sale. (It is true that stock prices reflect the prospects for future earnings, rather than invested capital; but investment helps to create the future earnings.) If such earnings were taxed in full to the stockholder at the time of reinvestment, the increment to stock values resulting from this should not later be taxed again as a capital gain. With the partial integration of corporate and personal taxes here recommended, double taxation could be avoided only by crediting the taxpayer with taxes paid by the corporation on gains attributable to reinvestment. Applying the credit mechanism will be a difficult administrative task.

Some capital gains are due to changes in the general price level (inflation). It is often claimed that these are illusory increases in value and should not be taxed, but this argument loses weight when the distribution of benefits and injuries from a rise in the price level (benefiting in general those holding stocks and real estate) is taken into account. Gains due to improvement in the prospects of particular investments are sometimes the result of a shrewd investment and sometimes merely a windfall. Gains may be obtained from short-term stock-market operations or may accrue gradually because of the plowing back of profits in a long-term investment. Unfortunately, quantitative data showing the importance of these various classes are limited and unsatisfactory. Capital losses originate like capital gains, and, as is usually the case with losses, their importance is rarely fully appreciated.

4. ALTERNATIVE TREATMENTS

Three major alternatives for the treatment of capital gains and losses will be discussed briefly. These are (1) to ignore such gains and losses (with qualifications), which is the British treatment; (2) to treat these increments and decrements like other income; and (3) to retain the present American system of classification as to the period the assets have been held, with application of a maximum rate to long-term gains and losses, and with segregation of losses so that these may be offset only against similar gains. Some modification of these major types of treatment will also be considered.

A. *Ignoring Capital Gains and Losses*

It is plausibly contended that the inclusion of capital gains in the income-tax base has increased the riskiness of investments without adding much to revenue in the long run. Moreover, the revenue that does result is unstable because of the wide fluctuations in capital gains from year to year. It is also argued that the taxation of capital gains has a perverse effect upon the stock market, accentuating the booms and depressions in the value of stocks. With perhaps more validity it is contended that the "liquidity of stocks" (the readiness with which they can be exchanged for cash or other investments) is lessened by the capital-gains tax, since recipients of large incomes hesitate to dispose of their holdings when the government claims such a large share of the gains that are realized. The social interest in liquidity is debatable, but a case for it can be made on the ground that those who have been successful with once-risky investments should not be deterred from shifting their capital to other new undertakings. Great Britain is cited as an instance where the taxation of capital gains has (with important qualifications) been avoided.

On the other hand, capital gains are closely related to other forms of income, and they are an important element in the distribution of economic power. These two facts create a presumption in favor of their being included in the income-tax base. Reinvested corporate income, as previously noted, may be transferred to the stockholder in the form of a capital gain. A discount on a bond is a substitute for interest to be paid. In the case of a corporation, the buying and selling of securities are often closely integrated with the other business of the concern; and, even in the case of individuals, the difference between buying and selling as a business and doing so as an investment avocation is rather artificial. And it is doubtful that a tax on capital gains with full allowance for capital losses offers any greater impediment to investment than the closely related tax on dividends.

The British treatment of capital gains and losses under the income tax started with a definition of income as being those receipts which are likely to recur periodically. Capital gains, along with some other receipts, were regarded as "casual" and thus excluded from the tax base. This doctrine was severely criticized by the Royal Commission of 1920, particularly since it applied to nonrecurring operations of a trading nature. Following the Commission's report, administrative and legal interpretation were modified to include in operating profit (as distinguished from capital gains) profit on transactions incident to a trade or business. The British system is defended on grounds similar to those presented above. It is emphasized, especially, that the receipts from the British income tax have been much more stable than our own and that, while capital gains are by no means the sole cause of this difference, they are an important cause. The British system is criticized on the ground that its classification is essentially arbitrary and that it affords opportunities for tax evasion. A number of devices are available for the conversion of dividends and interest into tax-free capital gains; and, in some cases, rent, wages, and salaries can likewise be converted into tax-free receipts.

B. *Treatment like Other Income*

The treatment of capital gains and losses like other income is advocated on the ground that this is the simplest and most equitable procedure. Doubt is expressed that the many and intricate developments in capital-gains taxation are an improvement over the simple procedure found in the primitive stages of the income-tax law. Compared with the present provisions, treatment like other income would grant the tax-taxpayer full and unconditional allowance for his losses, which, on the theory that losses figure heavily in incentives, would offer strong support for new investment. The proposal would, nevertheless, tend to increase the tax by applying the full (as distinct from a reduced maximum) rate to gains. Reducing top surtax rates in the general income would, of course, make this treatment more reasonable and acceptable.

Chief objection to treating capital gains and losses like other income is the previously cited contention that it would reduce the liquidity of stocks and adversely affect risk-bearing investment. It is argued, too, that, when capital gains result from corporate reinvestment, a capital-gains tax involves double taxation. This would be true if the corporate and personal taxes were integrated and a provision were made for a special levy (or advance payment) on undistributed earnings, with no credit allowed for this tax when gains were realized. Moreover, capital gains and losses accrue over different lengths of time, and it is argued that their realization and taxation in one year may throw the taxpayer's income into the higher brackets, thus working a hardship upon him.

1. *With Modifications*

If capital gains and losses are to be treated like other income, two modifications might be considered. One is to take into account the length of time involved in the accrual of the gain or loss. This can be done by dividing the gain or loss by the years of accrual, deriving an effective rate by adding the yearly accrual to the taxpayer's current income from other sources, calculating the additional (or reduced) tax resulting from this, and applying this effective rate to the entire capital gain or loss.[1] The whole problem of irregular personal income, of which capital gains are only a part, should, how-

---

[1] Thus, if Mr. Jones receives $10,000 in salary in 1942 and makes a capital gain of $100,000 on securities held for 10 years, the tax rate on one-tenth of that capital gain would be that regularly applying to the top half of a $20,000 income [$10,000 salary $+ \frac{1}{10}$ ($100,000) $=$ $20,000 income]. The same tax rate would then be applied to the entire capital gain. Instead of the current year's income, the average income for the last 5 years might be used in determining the beginning of the marginal rate to apply on a long-term capital gain (that is, on an investment held, say, 5 years or more).

ever, be reexamined for a fundamental solution. It is true that several schemes of averaging income have been tried without much success, but the injustices of annual accounting are often so flagrant that further effort in this direction is needed.

The second modification would adapt the capital-gains procedure to the system of integrated personal and corporate taxes recommended by the author. The proposal would eliminate the element of duplication in these taxes by allowing the stockholder a credit for corporate taxes on undistributed profits when he realizes a capital gain or loss. This procedure is clearly justified in theory. It simply applies to capital gains the principle that the taxes paid by the corporation should be credited to the recipient of corporate dividends when these dividends are distributed. From the standpoint of the stockholder, a capital gain attributable to corporate reinvestment is the equivalent of a liquidating dividend and should be entitled to the same credit as other delayed dividends. The allowance of such a credit in the case of capital gains does present administrative difficulties. It would involve the tabulation of the net taxed reinvestment per share during periods of stock-ownership and of the taxes paid by the corporation (advanced for the stockholder) on these sums.[1] If short cuts or rules of thumb for the sake of simplicity are considered necessary, they should approximate as closely as possible the objective here

---

[1] The operation of the tax credit to the stockholder for taxes advanced by the corporation on undistributed earnings is indicated in the following example: Mr. *A* pays $100 for a share of stock in a corporation. While he holds his stock, the corporation accumulates undistributed earnings before taxes totaling $50 for each share of stock. If the rate of tax on corporation profits is 20 per cent, the corporation pays the government $10 and retains $40 per share out of these earnings. Mr. *A* sells his share of stock for $145. He reports a capital gain of $55 on this transaction, for he has gained $45 plus the $10 tax paid on his share of undistributed profits by the corporation. The latter amount is worth $10 to him because he may deduct it from his tax.

Where Corporation *X* reinvests for a corporate shareholder *Y* and a personal stockholder of the latter realizes a capital gain, the calculation would proceed as though *Y*'s stockholder were *X*'s.

sought. One such rule that might be considered would be to exempt capital gains on common stock from half the normal tax. This would be a compromise in the interests of simplicity. Capital gains not due to reinvestment would be undertaxed, and those due to reinvestment would be overtaxed. The distribution of the reduction as among large and small taxpayers would be reasonable.

In the interests of both equity and simplicity, transfers at death and by gift should be treated as realizations by decedents and donors at market values current at the time of transfer.

C. *Special Classification with Maximum Rate and Segregation of Losses*

The third alternative, the present treatment of gains and losses, is essentially a compromise between the other two, and it is criticized on that account. The feature especially resented by investors is the segregation of losses with the provision that they may be offset only against similar gains. Under the present law as it now stands, many taxpayers feel that the government is guilty of sharp practice in taxing their gains and ignoring their losses. One-way rules usually cause resentment, and there is a strong presumption against them. (Another case of this kind is the rule that gain on the sale of a residence is taxable whereas loss on the same type of transaction is not deductible.) This criticism is strengthened by the fact that gains and losses are likely to be realized in different years and that available evidence shows a low correlation in the realization of gains and losses. Consequently, the possibility of offsetting one against the other is slight in many cases, a contingency only partly relieved by the more generous carry-over of losses now allowed. Unlimited deduction privileges would override the fact that capital losses are subject to some control and that they are often an aspect of investment exchanges involving no effect on income available for consumption. Against these considerations must be set the good will of the taxpayer, which could be had by more nearly equal treatment for losses, and the important stimulant for risk-taking incentives that would be provided by such a tax change.   Moreover, broadening the period for reckoning taxable income (proposed and discussed later) would itself reduce the danger of tax avoidance through manipulation of the realization of losses.

The author's conclusions concerning the taxation of capital gains and losses were submitted at the beginning of this chapter.   They call for the treatment of losses like other negative income—that is, for the elimination of segregation—and for generous carry-over privileges.   They call for due allowance for the time factor involved in the accrual of capital gains and for elimination of duplication in taxing gains attributable to the reinvestment of corporated income.   They call also for reduction in the higher surtax rates to make risk-bearing investments attractive to persons with large incomes.   These are conditions essential to the main recommendation that capital gains and losses should be treated like other income. Until these basic changes are made in our tax system, there will be need for special treatment of capital gains to encourage risky investment by persons with large incomes and to prevent injustice to those with large gains concentrated in particular years.

IX. MITIGATION OF DISCRIMINATION AGAINST IRREGULAR INCOME

1. CAUSE FOR ACTION

AN ATTEMPT should be made to eliminate or at least to mitigate the present tax discrimination against fluctuating personal income. Under the tax system as it now operates, a married person with two dependents whose net income alternates between nothing and $10,000 will pay about 50 per cent more in taxes over the years than a person with similar dependents whose net income remains constant at $5000. This is obviously bad both from the standpoint of equity and from the standpoint of incentives for risky enterprise. "Moreover, annual income-tax accounting makes crucially important for Treasury and taxpayer many hard (or impossible) questions as to the precise allocation of income between years—questions which lead to interminable disputes, hearings, and litigation and which, under a good system, would be of no real importance to either party."[1] Classifying some gains as casual (nonrecurrent) and excluding them from income taxation on that account, as in the British practice, takes hold of the problem at the wrong end. Almost all gains are casual in some degree. Casual gains should be taxed, but with due regard for their casual character.

2. EXPERIENCE WITH AVERAGING

Unfortunately, experience with various schemes of averaging has not been very encouraging. Mention has been made of the British experience, which finally abandoned averaging in favor of a carry-over system for losses. Much the same thing occurred in Wisconsin, where a system of averaging was

---

[1] Henry C. Simons, memorandum submitted to the author.

applied from 1927 to 1934 and then abandoned, leaving in its stead a carry-over of business losses.

In both the above instances, the main objection to averaging was that it frequently required the taxpayer to pay taxes on a base (or with a measure) which was several years "cold." This proved especially burdensome during depression periods when many incomes were low. Other objections were made to the administrative inconvenience of securing a back file of income-tax returns when a person moved from one reporting district to another and of obtaining a basis for averaging when his income in some years fell below the level required for reporting. Embarrassment also arose in determining how to weight the years before or after the taxpayer's income-creating activity—before he got a job or after he retired, withdrew from the country, or died.

3. PROPOSED SYSTEM OUTLINED

What is most needed is to give the taxpayer with fluctuating income some refuge from graduated rates applicable to the years when he has a high income and yet not fall into the error of simply shifting the payment of the tax to his low-income years. This could be done readily by permitting the taxpayer to sum his taxes over a period of years, calculate what his tax bill would have been if his income had been distributed evenly among these years, determine the difference between the two, and claim the difference as a refund or tax credit. To prevent minor refunds, the refund or credit might be limited to cases where the actual taxes exceeded the calculated taxes by 5 or 10 per cent.[1] The taxpayer might be permitted thus to average the income of any 5 or 10 successive years at his option, subject to the limitation that no year could appear in more than one averaging computation. The 5 or 10 per cent margin would exclude a large number of small transactions and is suggested for administrative convenience. The higher figure might be used in the case of 10-year averaging and the lower in case the

[1] The major features of this proposal were suggested by Henry C. Simons.

5-year period is chosen. Some administrative difficulties in this procedure could be reduced by establishing rules that income prior to the first year of filing or after the death of the taxpayer should be disregarded and that claims for a refund or offset should be contingent upon provision by the taxpayer of information necessary to establish his case. Changes in exemption status and tax rates would add a complication, but not a prohibitive one.

This system would involve some loss of revenue in bad years, but this drawback is far less significant than the gains in fairness and for incentives that the change would ensure. Admitting the difficulties in any scheme of averaging, one may nevertheless conclude that an attempted refinement of income-tax procedure along the lines above suggested is definitely worth a trial. Even a crude beginning should produce the needed experience upon which further refinements could be based.

A simplified procedure that would reduce administrative complication might be considered, especially if the income tax were to be broadened. This would be to allow a carry-over of unused personal exemptions in the lowest brackets of income and to confine the averaging and refunding privileges to intermediate and high brackets of income. Since business losses and capital losses would be subject to carry-over in any event, this proposal would allow the lower brackets most, if not all, of the advantages of averaging.

In the case of corporations, the injustices arising from irregularity can be alleviated quite effectively by a system of carrying losses forward and backward. This would be especially true if no attempt were made to apply a graduated rate to corporate income and no specific exemption were allowed.

4. PROBLEM OF SIMPLIFICATION

It is customary in reports on the income tax to remark that this levy can and should be drastically simplified. It is said, and rightly, that it is hardly consonant with democracy to have tax laws intelligible only to (some) tax lawyers and (some) tax specialists. The author shares this view, and yet he realizes that he has made suggestions which would add complications to the tax laws. Simplicity, like other interests in taxation, can be bought at too high a price. Fortunately, there are many points in the tax system where greater simplicity can be had at a reasonable cost or at no cost whatever. It is questionable whether or not the highly arbitrary earned-income credit[1] is worth its weight in complication, and it is quite clear that the division between normal taxes and surtaxes is an anachronism which serves no useful purpose. (Presumably the present weird combination of victory tax, normal tax, and surtax will be reduced to simpler and fewer elements before the war is finished.) Progress in simplified reporting is now being made and can be developed further. A trend toward a sound structural basis would in itself be a move toward simplicity and stability in the income tax. It is a bad theory that identifies increasing complication with progress.

[1] Since this was written, the 1944 act has eliminated the earned-income credit.

X. OVERHAULING DEATH TAXATION

THE question has been raised as to whether the death tax might not be overhauled to increase its effectiveness, thus compensating for some loss of revenue and distributive equality involved in a reduction of higher income surtaxes. This substitution could be supported on the basis that the death tax affects business incentives less than the surtax. Most of the interests in producing to accumulate a fortune, except certain acquisitive ambitions for one's family, are undisturbed by the death tax. Although death taxes cut heavily into the supply of available capital, no shortage in saving as such is anticipated. The shortage, if any, is in risk-seeking capital; and while inherited funds may be employed in this role, the likelihood is less than when such funds are in the hands of the original founder of the fortune.

For many years economists have proclaimed the strong social and economic grounds for death taxation. A classic summary of this view by John Stuart Mill reads as follows:[1]

The inequalities of property which arise from unequal industry, frugality, perseverance, talents, and to a certain extent even opportunities, are inseparable from the principle of private property, and if we accept the principle, we must bear with these consequences of it; but I see nothing objectionable in fixing a limit to what anyone may acquire by the mere favor of others, without any exercise of his faculties, and in requiring that if he desires any further accession of fortune he shall work for it.

It is wholesome for society to regard the builder of a fortune as a trustee who administers a sector of the country's wealth in the interests of the economy. He has demonstrated his capacity for this role by his success in the ordeal of competition;

[1] John Stuart Mill, *Principles of Political Economy.* Longmans, Green & Co., New York, 1923 Edition, p. 228.

but it does not follow that the virtues of the fortune builder are passed on to his heirs or that the corresponding responsibilities should be lodged with them. Many who have founded fortunes have been the first to recognize the soundness of this view. Equality of opportunity, which means more widely spread opportunity and incentive for enterprise, is promoted by death taxation.

Those opposing high death taxes claim that the family interest is a factor in incentives not to be underrated. In closely held corporations, a forced liquidation of stock following the death of a controlling stockholder may cause considerable disruption to the business. It is argued, moreover, that the death tax is a deterrent to investments in risk-bearing securities because it induces estate owners to shift their investments into liquid assets. The shift is made in anticipation of the need for cash to pay death taxes without a hasty, forced, and losing liquidation of assets. From the standpoint of the social interest, it is desirable that this situation should be avoided since owners of large estates are particularly qualified to assume the risk-bearing function for society. It is true that the federal government usually allows an extension of time in which the administrator of an estate can make necessary dispositions and that such extensions have not often been requested. But this alone is not proof that the estates tax exerts no unfortunate pressure upon owners to seek greater liquidity in their investments. To meet this objection, consideration might be given to the possibility of evaluating assets for death tax purposes according to their value at death or the amount realized in disposition (or liquidation), whichever is lower.[1] This would require some safeguards, but it would largely eliminate the present pressure on the pattern of estate investment and thus prevent losses in settling estates. Since the death tax is so set up that disposition on a large scale is frequently necessary, this change would also be in the interests of equity.

[1] A step in this direction was taken when the government allowed the executor to elect evaluation of the property in the estate as of 1 year after the decedent's death. This provision can be liberalized.

Consideration of incentives for risk-taking and enterprise would support a reduction in income surtaxes and an increase in death taxes. It is not necessary, however, to raise federal estates-tax rates (already among the highest in the world) in order to increase the effectiveness of the tax. It has long been recognized that, in spite of very high rates and occasional onerous burdens imposed by the federal estates-tax law, the results of the death tax system are fiscally disappointing and its impact highly capricious. Without venturing to supply any great detail, the following observations are offered for consideration:

1. The estates tax should be integrated with the gift tax. Capricious and undesirable results follow from the fact that, for example, the owner of an estate of $100,000 can make a 90 per cent saving by disposing of his estate through *inter vivos* gifts.

2. Notorious loopholes, particularly those relating to the disposition of property by means of trusts, are in urgent need of repair.

3. Better coordination of federal and state taxes, with due regard for the elimination of multiple taxation, is needed.

4. Exemption of $60,000 at a time of urgent revenue need is, to say the least, unwise.[1]

5. Exemptions, and perhaps rates, should be differentiated according to the relationship of the heir to the deceased.

It is recognized that the death tax field is highly intricate, with many possibilities for discriminatory anomalies. It is important to make the tax more equitable as well as more productive. Again the example of the British is likely to prove helpful, although they have badly neglected loopholes associated with gifts. At all events, the British, with lower top rates than ours, have succeeded in making their death tax system relatively much more productive.

---

[1] Of course, both the social and the personal interest in provision for the security of dependent relatives must be recognized. For this and other reasons, widows and minor children of deceased estate owners are entitled to special consideration.

Both the income and the death tax involve complex mechanisms as well as difficult administrative and avoidance problems. It is evident, however, that many of these complexities are not inherent, and they can be resolved with adequate effort. This must be done because, unless these complexities and difficulties are held within reasonable bounds, simpler but less equitable and less economically desirable forms of taxation will have to be substituted.

XI. SPECIAL EXCISES AND GENERAL
SALES TAXES

Postwar federal sales taxes, especially those involving a levy on the necessities of life, are undesirable. They are objectionable from the standpoint of equity since they fall most heavily upon low-income families. Because they do not involve the personal discipline incident to direct taxes, they are conducive to governmental extravagance. In preference to general sales taxes, high special excises are a tolerable, even though not a desirable, substitute for adequate standard rates in the personal income tax.

We have already noted the strong trend toward business taxation in the federal tax system and have recommended that this trend should be reversed. This raises sharply the question of alternatives: What kind of revenue system should we establish? The proposals here made look in the direction of a more personal tax system. It would be possible, however, to move in the opposite direction—toward an impersonal, indirect, consumption-tax system. If this were the goal, the proper procedure would probably be to retain business taxes but to broaden their base. Instead of using net income as the base of the business tax, we could use net operating income (interest not deductible), or "value added," or gross income. Perhaps eventually we should arrive at retail-sales taxation as the mainstay of federal revenues.

A consumption-tax system has vigorous supporters, and it can be defended with some plausible arguments. It looks particularly desirable on the score of business incentives. The main alternative, taxation of net income, does affect incentives for enterprise adversely. This result is magnified if the tax is levied on a progressive scale and further magnified if the progression is carried to excess. While it is probably not possible to base a tax system on unproductiveness and failure, a consumption-tax system goes a long way in this direction. Finally, there is the traditional "advantage of consumption taxes—ease of payment and ease of collection."

Nevertheless, it seems to us that there are conclusive objections to a shift toward consumption taxes in the postwar revenue system. The inequity of such levies is too obvious and too generally recognized to require analysis. Furthermore, this form of taxation leads most readily to governmental extravagance. The discipline involved in the payment of direct personal taxes makes for awareness of taxes and a demand for restraint in the conduct of government. It was not accidental that Townsend chose a sales tax to pave the way for his old-age pension program. Public budgets should be scrutinized as carefully and with as much proprietary interest as private budgets. Of course, the tax system is not the only element affecting the development of such public attention, but it is a factor of much importance. Finally, the maintenance of adequate consumer demand—particularly for the economic goods that have a high social value—is threatened by a tax system that seeks a disproportionate part of its revenue from the lowest levels of income. The states, with their more limited fiscal resources, will probably maintain and perhaps develop further the consumption-tax field. At all events, their tax systems are likely to remain predominantly regressive. The federal government should stress direct personal taxation.

Retention of some special excises—such as those on liquor and tobacco—is likely, and these taxes, if not the best, are a tolerable element in the federal tax system. The taxation of liquor, even though the demand is inelastic, is not so objectionable, at least, as the taxation of bread and salt. The former leaves the taxpayer an alternative to the tax that is quite compatible with the national interest.

The excises provide the federal tax system with an additional element of diversity. It would probably be rash, and certainly unprecedented, to rely on the personal income tax to produce, say, 80 per cent of the revenue that will be required after the war. Yet some relief for postwar taxpayers in the lower income brackets will be justified; and, as between excises and the standard income-tax rates, the former are the better area for concessions. The elaborate system and substantial yields of wartime excise taxation make possible considerable relief from these taxes without entirely eliminating the more defensible levies. If during the war the federal government launches upon a general sales-tax program, these levies should be the first to go when the war ends.

XII. EXPERIENCE (MERIT) RATING IN PAY ROLL TAXES FOR UNEMPLOYMENT

DURING the thirties there was considerable support for "incentive taxation," a term used to describe the deliberate use of taxation to encourage desirable economic activity and to discourage undesirable economic activity or passivity. Taxes on idle capacity and hoarding were recommended to replace those on production and investment. A more detailed study of these proposals is contemplated for our final report. Here the opinion may be expressed that probably a sound and sensible tax system is as practical a program of encouraging production with incentive taxation as is likely to be found. However, taxation may also be applied as an incentive for business management to choose production policies desirable from the standpoint of social interests other than those bearing on maximum production. A differential pay roll tax for unemployment compensation is a measure of this character. Under the title of "experience rating," this form of differential is now provided by the unemployment compensation systems of a majority of the states. But it is threatened by the opposition of the Social Security Board, whose effort to nationalize the unemployment compensation program includes abolition of experience rating.

Experience rating undertakes to apportion the cost of unemployment compensation in some degree according to the achievements of industries and firms in avoiding unemployment. The system has long been used in workmen's compensation, where it has played a substantial part in reducing industrial accidents and occupational diseases. True, unemployment is less within the control of business management than are accidents; but management is far from a negligible factor in either instance, and, in the case of unemployment, it can be particularly effective in reducing seasonal layoffs. Apart from the interest in preventing unemployment, there is an advantage in distributing a social cost to the production with which it is associated. It is appropriate, too, that a business should assume some responsibility for the regular maintenance of its labor supply. If business is required to pay a dismissal wage to its employees, it might at least be allowed the privilege of using its ingenuity to reduce this social cost. It is true that experience rating and state unemployment compensation systems stand in the way of a comprehensive national system of social security, supported out of one big fund fed by a single system of taxes. But a centralized and undifferentiated "insurance" program would tend to obliterate the remaining lines of individual and business responsibility in the social security system and might become a gigantic system of charity. Against experience rating as a basis for a differential unemployment tax stands the fact that it can be abused as a pretext for undermining standards. For example, it appears that experience-rating states have, in some cases, unduly restricted the qualifications establishing the eligibility of employees to benefits.[1] Space does not permit further excursion into this field except to voice the opinion that experience rating in unemployment compensation deserves a much fairer and longer trial than it has yet received and that neither the state nor the federal government should intervene to cut the trial short.

[1] See Ewan Clague and Ruth Reticker, "Trends in Disqualification from Benefits under State Unemployment Compensation Laws," *Social Security Bulletin*, Vol. VII, January, 1944, pp. 12–23.

XIII. SPECIAL TAXATION PROBLEMS OF THE WAR RELATED TO RECONVERSION

WHILE this book is mainly concerned with taxation in the postwar period, certain aspects of wartime taxation have a direct bearing on the postwar problem. Some of these have been mentioned, and some recommendations have been made regarding them. In treating corporate losses and the excess-profits tax, attention was called to the present generous carry-back of losses and the excess-profits-tax credit introduced in 1942. A continuation of these provisions as long as the effects of the war upon business remain important was recommended. For this purpose, a 3-year carry-back might be more appropriate than the present 2-year period. Some restrictions on manipulation of expenditures (as in the case of advertising campaigns) would be needed to prevent waste and unfairness in the carry-back period. It is true that a long carry-back period would involve some offsetting against war income of losses and unused credits which would not be attributable to the war. On the other hand, the longer period would allow a more complete coverage of costs directly due to the war. Probably 2 years would cover most of these expenses; but some, such as inventory losses, might not be incurred until later. In addition, the 3-year carry-back would spread the demand for and availability of reconversion capital over a longer time. However, the retention of the present postwar provisions is much more important than their extension, and the latter is not recommended.

The situation will probably call for retention of the carry-back feature of the excess-profits tax after the tax itself is suspended. This might seem unduly generous to prosperous corporations, but it is based mainly on the eminently sound principle that war-profits taxes should be applied to actual and not fictitious war earnings.[1]

To illustrate the operation of the present carry-backs, if Corporation *A* has earned large excess profits and has paid high excess-profits taxes throughout the war period but, because of repercussions of the war, barely makes ends meet in the first 2 years after the war, the returns of the last 2 war years may be reopened. The difference between the actual postwar earnings and the maximum earnings that would not be subject to the excess-profits tax may, in effect, be deducted from the income of the war years. This would entitle the company to a refund. The same would be true if Corporation *A* had incurred a loss after the war, except that in this case the wartime net income tax return as well as the excess-profits tax liability might be reopened. To some degree the system provides that the experience of the postwar years may be averaged with that of the war years in the ultimate determination of war income and profits taxes.

The carry-backs will provide corporations with considerable postwar capital, but, unfortunately, not when they need it most. The same is true of the postwar 10 per cent excess-profits-tax refund, since the bonds representing claims to this refund do not become negotiable until the cessation of hostilities. The Treasury has recommended that the carry-back allowances shall be made available (at least as an offset against accrued tax liability) upon submission of adequate evidence establishing a reasonable expectation of eligibility for such allowances. In addition, the Treasury might be authorized and instructed to grant the 10 per cent refunds to taxpayers who can present reasonable evidence of their need for reconversion funds before the end of the war.

There has been considerable discussion of the possibility and

[1] "Assuming that war is something of an abnormality, a special excursion which business has been obliged to take, it tends to follow that both the cost of coming and going should be charged to war revenue." William A. Paton, letter to the author.

wisdom of allowing further reserve deductions for postwar contingencies. The carry-back system, if retained, will offer substantial consideration for postwar contingencies; but, except for corporations that operate at a loss, it provides no retroactive postwar relief from high war taxes other than the excess-profits tax.

Corporations are now permitted to deduct, as expenses, charges in connection with certain reserves, such as depreciations; and a similar allowance for postwar contingencies suggests itself. The difficulty here is that many of the contingencies are so unpredictable that it is practically impossible to determine accurately how large reserves for them ought to be. Contingencies will differ from industry to industry, and even from company to company within the same industry. They may involve plant, equipment, inventories, and labor and assume countless forms within these categories. On the face of it, it seems impossible to allow income tax deductions for contingency reserves when so large a factor of uncertainty is involved.

Two alternative means of dealing with this situation have been suggested. The first calls for a reserve optional with the company of some proportion of the company's net income. This reserve is to be available for a large variety of war-caused postwar expenditures; if it is not so used, it is to revert to the income of the years from which it is taken. The second alternative calls for a carry-back of net war-caused postwar expenditures incurred within a limited period of time. This contemplates some balancing of positive against negative items. For example, a concern may have some equipment the value of which has suffered from accelerated obsolescence during the war but other equipment, acquired during the war and fully amortized, which is still useful. The two classifications would be considered together in determining true war profits. The second alternative would probably be attended by more strict accounting than the first. Both would involve great, but probably not prohibitive, difficulty in distinguishing war-caused from other expenditures. Consideration should be given to the feasibility of modifying the present carry-back system so that war-caused expense of the postwar period might be offset directly against war income.

Provision for war-caused postwar expenditures need not interfere with the development of sound tax procedures allowing the deduction of specific reserves for specific contingencies. For example, an inventory-reserve deduction both for war and peacetime application would have many advantages. An increase in the value of an inventory held by a business due to an increase in prices is actually an unrealized capital gain and is not a proper subject for taxation. Realized inventory profits which must be reinvested in a new stock of goods at higher prices than those realized on goods replaced afford the taxpayer no means with which to pay taxes. These inventory profits could appropriately be set aside as an accounting reserve to compensate for prospective losses at the time when prices move in the opposite direction. An inventory reserve would be as useful to discount business-cycle changes as it would be to discount fictitious profits arising out of the war. Unfortunately, inventory-reserve accounting for tax purposes involves administrative difficulties that have thus far prevented its adoption.[1] Another case where a specific reserve, with proper safeguards, seems desirable and feasible is that of postwar dismissal compensation. The Treasury has recommended allowance for such a reserve.

The opinion has also been expressed in this book that our present (1942) standard personal income tax rates are little if any above the level required by prewar revenue needs and that accordingly they are much too low for the present emergency. Higher taxes would, among other things, relieve the pressure on prices. Unless prices are kept in bounds, the deferred purchasing power vital to postwar prosperity will be dissipated.

[1] The development of "last-in, first-out" inventory accounting and its acceptance for tax purposes has reduced but not eliminated the need for inventory reserves.

XIV. FISCAL POLICY IN THE POSTWAR PERIOD

CERTAIN aspects of postwar fiscal policy related to tax policy require at least brief comment in this report.

1. BUDGETS AND DEBTS

Should we balance the budget annually, cyclically, or not at all? Should we amortize the debt, add to it, or maintain it at the present level? Although calculations of yields from particular rates are not presented here,[1] some general observations concerning adequacy of yield are in order. First of all, the budget must be balanced when the economy is operating at reasonably high levels of income and employment, and it should at times produce a surplus. In other words, cyclical deficits and surpluses are not to be shunned. This does not imply, however, that stability of revenue is of secondary importance; and our recommendations have taken this factor into account. Whether or not we should go further than to balance the budget during the immediate postwar years depends entirely on the success with which we attain high economic levels during this period. These high economic levels are more important than debt retirement, but it may be possible to achieve both. The policy of reducing fixed charges, in accord with long-standing American tradition, is supported by the very real interest in the elasticity of the public credit, a factor that may be important in future emergencies.

2. COUNTERCYCLE INFLUENCE OF TAXATION

If tax rates are not increased during a depression, taxation automatically exercises a countercycle influence. This is the sort of countercycle taxation policy which is likely to prove

[1] These calculations will be presented in the detailed final report.

most practical. The taxation program outlined here will, on the whole, apply to all phases of the business cycle. Some special stimulants and narcotics might be needed, however, in case of extreme fluctuations. These remedies should be associated with the factor of investment.

An appropriate tool to use as an investment control would be a special allowance of accelerated depreciation during extreme depression years.[1] This would encourage improvements and reduce current tax obligations during bad years, and it would exercise reverse or compensating effects during good years. As previously stated, tools of this character should be reserved for extreme conditions.

3. AVOIDING INFLATION

Many feel that, at the close of the war and for some time at least, our major problem will be one of price control and that tax reductions would have an unfortunate inflationary influence. In consideration of this possibility, some flexibility in the timing of reductions has been recommended. Moreover, it is possible that rapid reconversion of business will curb inflation as effectively as any other program, and it is by no means certain that inflation will be a problem.

4. TIMING OF TAX REDUCTIONS IN THE POSTWAR PERIOD

There is no clear consensus of prediction as to the pattern of postwar economic events. Nevertheless, it is possible to outline a probable pattern and to suggest the objectives of taxation and the appropriate taxation program that would attend each phase. This is outlined on page 103.

[1] See p. 65.

Fiscal Policy in the Postwar Period

Period	Economic Characteristics	Taxation Measures
Phase 1		
Less than a year following the end of the war	Inflationary: supply of civilian goods lags behind demand Production handicapped by shifting markets and other reconversion problems Attitude: some diffidence due to transitional unemployment and uncertainty as to the future Business capital: short in some places	Repeal the excess-profits tax to become effective a year later. This will take no chances on premature lifting of controls and will promote confidence Reduce the corporate tax conservatively
Phase 2		
A year or two	Deflationary: production handicapped by shifting markets, other readjustments after rehabilitation period Attitude: considerable diffidence	Excess-profits-tax repeal to become effective except that carry-back provisions are retained Tax system is repaired for peacetime basis—corporate and personal taxes are fully integrated; excise taxes are revised downward drastically
Phase 3		
Several years	Inflationary Business and consumer confidence returns	No further reduction and perhaps some increases in certain taxes (social security or personal income taxes) Use of surplus revenues, if any, to retire indebtedness

XV. CONSIDERATION OF OBJECTIONS
TO THE TAX MODIFICATIONS
HERE PROPOSED

ANTICIPATION and consideration of certain objections that may be offered to our proposed tax modifications seem desirable.

The program might be criticized as too favorable for business and too hard on the lower income brackets. With the exception, perhaps, of the reduction in highest surtaxes—a concession to moderation—all the recommendations are quite as defensible in terms of equity as in those of incentive. The proposal to reduce surtaxes is balanced by that to strengthen death taxes. It is true that direct relief offered to the lower brackets is confined largely to mitigation of sales taxes (where it can be quite substantial) and to a possible conservative reduction in the standard rate of personal tax (depending mostly upon what happens to this rate before the end of the war). A shift from business to personal taxes, by bringing tax burdens into the open and by extending the scope of personal tax with its exemptions and progressive rates, will also benefit the recipients of lower incomes. Under the modifications here proposed, the tax system would be more widely and more positively progressive than it was before the war.

Some might criticize the program as inadequate to accomplish its objectives. Such critics will be proponents of consumption taxation, whose position has been considered and rejected in this report. Others might regret the absence of recommendations of special immunities and penalties believed to foster production and employment. Our one venture in this direction is to recommend certain concessions to small new enterprises, and this is intended to offset an unfair competitive handicap rather than to grant a special privilege. In addition, it is suggested that consideration should be given to accelerated depreciation and obsolescence allowances as a stimulant in periods of low economic activity. Other possible innovations of this sort are daring and otherwise attractive, but their soundness is more questionable. They can wait, in any event, until certain mistakes of this order already in the tax system have been corrected. Some support can be found for the view that employment and output can be promoted more effectively by relieving personal rather than corporate tax burdens. But our proposal may obversely be regarded as calling for a reduction in personal taxes to the extent that they overlap corporate taxes.

Still others might doubt the fiscal feasibility of our recommendations. The author believes that the program presented here is flexible enough to meet the demands of fiscal requirements. Moreover, any stimulative tax program is obliged to take some chances on the success of the venture. It aims at a broad tax base to obviate the necessity of excessive rates and other repressive features. Like risky enterprise itself, it necessarily involves some chances on the success of the innovations.

Further skepticism may be felt concerning the political feasibility of our proposals. The chief recommendation, namely, the integration of personal and corporate taxes, will be regarded by many as unacceptable to Congress. The popular idea that corporations possess ability to pay of the highest order may not be readily uprooted unless it is recognized that taxes cannot be borne by inanimate objects or by impersonal creatures of the law. These entities can make the payments; but the burdens of taxation fall on the owners, workers, or customers, in the form of reduced income or higher prices. To many observers, the corporation income tax would lose its benevolent mien if it were seen in its true light as a sales tax in disguise. But even if these fallacies remain to influence legislation, our recommendation should still be acceptable. It would leave the corporate tax in much its present form, eliminating only the factor of duplication. This modification has precedent not only in the British law but in earlier American procedure.

XVI. CONCLUSION

THE recommendations made in this report work toward a tax system without duplication of taxes, moderate as to degree, universal in application, and free from special privileges. The emphasis is placed on a direct personal tax to be measured by all income and to be paid by a large majority of American families.

What is needed is a tax program that will be conducive to high levels of production and employment in the postwar period and one that will appeal to Americans in all walks of life as equitable and well balanced. If this report contributes to the inauguration of such a program, it will have achieved its purpose.

A NOTE ON
THE COMMITTEE FOR ECONOMIC DEVELOPMENT
AND ITS RESEARCH PROGRAM

The Committee for Economic Development was organized in August, 1942, by a group of business leaders who were convinced that the attainment and maintenance of high employment after the war dare not be left to chance. To seize the opportunities for unprecedented peacetime prosperity in the postwar era and to avoid the real perils of mass unemployment or mass government employment, they believed that individual employers, while in no degree relaxing their efforts toward military victory, must begin to plan promptly, realistically, and boldly.

There is widespread agreement among economists that American prosperity after the war calls for the sustained employment of 7 to 10 million more workers than in 1940, our banner peacetime year hitherto. The only sound road to such increased employment is the enlargement of production and sales of goods and services to a level some 30 to 45 per cent higher than that of 1940. This means that businessmen must make their plans for postwar business on a greatly expanded basis as compared to any known peacetime year.

To assist them to make their maximum contribution toward this goal, the Committee for Economic Development has organized locally (as of May, 1944) in more than 1800 American communities in all states of the union. An estimated 40,000 businessmen are working as members of these committees to persuade and assist as many as possible of the nation's 2,000,000 private employers to begin now to plan their postwar production and employment schedules.

No pattern or over-all program is imposed on these local committees. Each is autonomous, since each understands the peculiar problems of its community better than can any outsider. Yet the problems they meet and the tools they need are in basic respects the same.

TxU

Therefore, tested procedures for making estimates of both postwar production and employment are supplied to them by the national C.E.D. office. In addition, the country's outstanding specialists in industrial management, in product design, in advertising and selling, and in training of sales personnel have placed their skills freely at the service of all cooperating businessmen, through handbooks, films, training courses, business clinics, and forums for the local committees.

To plan for the future, the businessman needs particularly some measure for estimating postwar demand for his individual product. Another important service of C.E.D. is its postwar market analysis, which is being conducted with the cooperation of many trade associations and leading industrial firms and will cover more than 500 finished-goods products.

Even with the best of tools the businessman knows he cannot be wholly successful in carrying out plans for postwar expansion unless national policies prevail that make business expansion possible. To describe and define what these national policies of government, business, and labor should be to encourage higher production and more jobs is the special task of the C.E.D. Research Division. This is the purpose of the research reports, of which this volume on taxation is the first.

To the long-range economic questions involved in this undertaking have been added the particular and hazardous economic problems arising out of the war. Both areas are being studied. It is hoped that the reports, as a unit, will provide the information that many have been seeking concerning problems intimately related to the life of each of us, as well as to the future of our society.

The authors of these reports have already won distinction in their own fields. Perhaps more important is the fact that their previous work has demonstrated not only the competence but the vigor of thought which these complex problems demand. Knowing, however, that the problems that would be scrutinized—taxation policy, monetary policy, international trade, demobilization of the war economy, and the like—are not separate ones, but are integrated and must be studied in relationship one to the other, the C.E.D. sought to make possible an exchange of information and views between the experts themselves.

What is probably a unique scheme of conferences was established, and it gives us hope that these C.E.D. reports and recommendations will help to close the gap between the world of expert knowledge and the world of practical application. A Research Committee consisting of representative successful businessmen was set up; to this group was added a Research Advisory Board whose members are recognized as among our leading social scientists; and finally, the persons who would be responsible for the individual reports were named, to comprise the Research Staff.

The subject matter of each report is discussed by the members of these three groups, meeting together. "Discussed" is an inadequate term. "Earnestly argued, and for long hours" does more justice to the work. The author of the report therefore has the benefit of criticism and suggestion by many other competent minds. He is able to follow closely the development of the reports on other economic matters that affect his own study.

No effort has been made to arrive at absolute agreement. There is no single answer to the problems that are being studied. What is gained is agreement as to the determinative factors in each problem, and the possible results to be achieved by differing methods of handling the problem. The author of the report has full responsibility, and complete freedom, for proposing whatever action or solution seems advisable to him. There is only one rule—the approach must be from the standpoint of the general welfare and not from that of any special economic or political group; the objective must be high production and high employment in a democratic society.

Since the author is free to present his own conclusions and does not speak for the Research Committee or for the Research

Advisory Board, the Research Committee will issue, for each study, where desirable, a separate C.E.D. *policy statement.* This may endorse all of the recommendations arrived at by the author, or it may disagree with some.

The research studies already under way divide roughly into two parts:

A. *The transition from war to peace:* the problems involved in the early *attainment* of high levels of employment and production when the war is over;

B. *The longer-term fundamental problems* involved in the *maintenance* of high levels of productive employment after the transition period has passed.

The subjects to be covered by the individual monographs in the two series are:

A. *The Transition from War to Peace:*

1. *Production, Jobs and Taxes* (the present volume).

2. *Lessons from World War I and Its Aftermath,* by Theodore O. Yntema and Martha Jane Marshall, of the C.E.D. Research Staff.

3. *Liquidating War Production,* including termination of war contracts, disposal of government-owned plants and surplus inventories. By A. D. H. Kaplan, Professor of Economics, University of Denver (on leave).

4. *Removing Wartime Economic Controls,* which studies questions concerning controls over production, transportation, manpower, wages and prices, profits, credit, consumption and other economic functions. By J. M. Clark, Professor of Economics, Columbia University.

5. *Financing the Reconversion and Expansion of Business,* especially in the crucial period of transition from wartime to peacetime economy. By Charles C. Abbott, Associate Professor of Business Economics, Harvard University.

6. *Manpower Demobilization and Reemployment*, indicating the nature of the problem, analyzing its different aspects and proposing appropriate policies and measures. By Robert R. Nathan, formerly Director of the Planning Committee, War Production Board.

7. *Providing for Transition Unemployment*, estimating the size and duration of the transition unemployment problem and the characteristics of the period which will affect unemployment policies. By Richard A. Lester, Associate Professor of Economics, Duke University.

8. *Money and Banking Policy During Transition*, especially in its relation to federal fiscal policy and the financial requirements of business enterprises for reconversion and expansion. By John K. Langum, Assistant Vice-president, Federal Reserve Bank of Chicago.

9. *Agriculture after the War*, especially the maintenance of a price level that will support steady high production. By T. W. Schultz, Professor of Agricultural Economics, University of Chicago.

10. *International Economic Relations in the Postwar World*, examining what kind of foreign trade policies and mechanisms we can adopt that will increase our gains from international trade without endangering world peace and without interfering with the full and stable employment of our national resources. By Calvin B. Hoover, Dean of the Graduate School of Arts and Sciences, Duke University. This study, as well as the two preceding it, will also have important implications for the longer run after the transition to a peace-time economy is completed.

B. *The Longer-term Fundamental Problems:*
1. *Providing Adequate Incentives for Enterprise.* By C. E. Griffin, Dean of the School of Business Administration, University of Michigan.
2. *Developing a Constructive Tax Policy*, a continuation of the present tax study into the period after the

transition and an enquiry also into the problems of state and local taxation. By Harold M. Groves, author of the present volume.

3. *Minimizing Business Fluctuation and Unemployment,* a series of studies which will be the major undertaking of the research staff during the coming year.

4. *The Special Problems of Small Business,* enquiring in detail into possible methods of assistance, both national and local.

These are the subjects so far authorized by the Research Committee of the C.E.D. Others will be undertaken from time to time. These subject titles will not necessarily be the same as the book titles when finally published.

INDEX